Life and Loves
of a
War Hero's Daughter

Copyright Christine Edney 2018

All rights reserved.

Contents

INTRODUCTION	1
MY JOURNEY	3
MY EARLY YEARS	17
BACK TO EMSWORTH	33
MALTA	47
BACK TO ENGLAND	57
NEW ZEALAND	85
AUCKLAND	89
EPILOGUE	111

INTRODUCTION

It was whilst I was sorting through boxes of memorabilia and photographs that I came across a photo of me with George Harrison. We were standing together outside his house in Liverpool, and it made me realise what a unique and unconventional life I've led and that my story needed to be told. I was 15 years old and, having spent my growing up years travelling from place to place, I had no idea what lay ahead of me. Unless your family were part of the armed forces, baby boomers like me did not usually have much opportunity for travel. We did not come into the 'rich' category either. Now in my late sixties, I often wonder what impact the experiences of my early life has had on my personality, character, and choices in life. A lot, I would imagine, although I also believe that the genes we inherit have a large part to play. My enthusiasm for photography has enabled me to look back on my life and to remember much that may have otherwise been lost. I was given my first camera aged nine and all my photographs have been carefully stored and transported with me on my journey through life.

I want to acknowledge the contribution my mother has made to this autobiography, for – without her elaborate stories and memories of our life – much would have been lost. Also, to my father for writing his own autobiography before he died in 2003, from which much of the naval history and detail has been extracted.

MY JOURNEY

It's June 1963. I'm fifteen years old and this was a year to remember in many ways, not least the day I met George Harrison at his house in Liverpool. We were enjoying another summer trip to visit my grandparents and catch up with relatives. It was Saturday and my nana was bustling around as usual, lighting the fire in the living room (it always seemed cold up north compared to our place in Sussex), washing some clothes, and pushing them through the mangle. She was making cups of tea for everyone when my sister Julia suddenly announced, "I've managed to get George Harrison's address! I want to go and visit him tomorrow. Will you come with me Christine?"

I was not as enthusiastic as Julia as it meant catching a bus on a Sunday morning and then possibly finding he wasn't even home. In the end I relented as she was most insistent that she would not go on her own. So, the following morning, we ventured down to catch the bus in the bright June sunshine, a journey of about twenty minutes to Woolton. As we were looking for 174 Mackets Lane, I kept thinking we shouldn't do this, not on a Sunday, not arriving unannounced. Eventually we found the house; a not very smart semi-detached house, albeit with a garage and short driveway in a tree-lined road. Nervously, we knocked at the front door and waited. The door swung open and a dark haired young guy stood there, who we presumed was George's brother, Pete.

"Sorry to bother you but is George at home?" we asked, shyly.

"Yes, come in," George's brother said with a friendly smile.

"George!" he yelled up the stairs "You've got a couple of visitors". He showed us into the living room and offered us a cup of tea, asking how far we had come. We chatted politely about various subjects, even mundane things such as the weather, when George suddenly appeared in the doorway, casually dressed. He looked as though he had just rolled out of bed. He seemed shy and came and sat down with his cup of something. The first thing I did was to apologise for arriving on a Sunday morning, unannounced. George didn't seem phased, he got his breakfast together on the table and we chatted whilst he ate it.

"I just got back from London last night," he said. "We were there doing a demo disc of our next single. Do you want to hear it?"

Enthusiastically we nodded our heads feeling very privileged that we were about to hear the new single in advance of production. The Beatles had already had a couple of hits including Please Please Me. This new one was called Love Me Do. After we had listened to it George said, "What do you think? Do you like it?"

"Oh yes!" we replied beaming, "it's wonderful".

After about an hour or so I felt we ought to politely say we needed to go. "Before we go," I said, "Would you mind if we had a photo taken with you outside the house, George?" He happily agreed to our request and we each had one taken individually with him. Pete then offered to drive us home. We were very glad to accept his offer and rushed into my grandmother's house to tell everyone about our unbelievable morning with one of The Beatles. We even had a photo to prove it!

It was just as well I had that photo of me and George because none of my school friends would have ever believed me.

As I travelled the world with my parents, my grandparents' house in Liverpool was my only stability, the home I knew would always be there - with a loving welcome. My safe-haven. The journey to Liverpool would take us two days, driving first to Birmingham where we would stay with relatives, then on to Liverpool the next day. I can still recall our old car trying to get up steep inclines and hills. The car would usually grind to a halt and we'd all have to get out and walk up the hill and meet Dad at the top. Me, Mum, my two sisters and brother, and the dog. Of course, there were no motorways, just winding lanes with no signs as they had been removed during the war to confuse the enemy. I don't know how we ever made it up there! On one occasion we were somewhere in the middle of the countryside when a puncture was noticed in the rear wheel.

"Oh no!" Dad exclaimed. "Everyone get out and help me get the luggage off the roof rack". We all tumbled out, lots of moans from the younger two, and after the luggage had been removed from the roof and placed on the roadside, Dad attempted to remove the punctured wheel with the jack. Unfortunately, the jack collapsed, and the axle was stuck on the ground! Dad attempted to walk to find the nearest garage, not easy when you don't know where you are, and it was getting dark. Luckily two farm workers came by and with the assistance of their tractor, managed to lift the car and put the spare wheel in position. The whole episode sounds like a comedy sketch these days, but it was no laughing matter then, I can tell you.

My first visit to Liverpool was in the summer of 1948 to celebrate my christening at All Saints Church, Stoneycroft. My maternal great-grandparents were there as well as numerous other relatives. We had a very large extended family and Mum was the only one who had left Liverpool for a life with a sea captain, so it was with great joy that she could return on a regular basis and reconnect with everyone.

My Christening day. Photo taken outside Nana's house in Anstey Road. Great - Grandma Sarah holding me, mum and nana behind

I was born in Southsea, on the 2nd day of a freezing February in 1948. However, I was nearly born in the tropics. My parents were living in Bermuda when I was conceived, and plans had been made for my birth on the island. Mother had even travelled to New York to acquire a beautiful cot and pram for the event. All was ready when my father was unexpectedly ordered to return to the UK with his ship, and his pregnant wife.

As a seven-month-old foetus, I travelled the first half of the journey in a 'rickety old plane' (mother's words) that nearly came down in a horrific thunderstorm! The rest of the journey was made on a banana boat, via Jamaica, where on more than one occasion Mum thought she was going to be attacked by the "natives"! Bananas had not been seen in England for over six years, so the arrival of a banana boat into Portsmouth would have been a welcoming sight, I imagine.

As Dad's ship was stationed in Portsmouth, a place to live was found in Southsea. The news at the time was reporting that the Lake District was to become a National Park and the latest dance craze was the Jitterbug, but that didn't concern me as I was being born in St. Mary's Nursing Home. Most babies at that time were born at home. It would be another six months before the NHS was launched so I must presume St. Mary's was a private nursing home. As was the advice in those days, it would be two weeks before Mum would be allowed home with me, and Dad was not allowed to touch or hold me until that time. For young mothers these days those rules sound somewhat bizarre. Yet disease was rife, and no chances could be taken. Little did I know for the next twenty-two years I would be moving house approximately every eighteen months. Altogether, I attended six different schools, and lived in four different countries.

By all reports, (which I like to believe) I was a beautiful baby – with olive skin and very dark hair. Everyone in the neighbourhood came out to see the pram that had been bought in New York, which Mum proudly pushed up and down the road, explaining to curious neighbours how she came to acquire it. Being born just after the end of the Second World War, everything was still on ration and it was difficult for people to even buy a pram, let alone one so grand! Rationing continued until 1953 and I still have my old ration book to this day.

Apart from being beautiful, I'm told I was a most compliant little baby. Mother stuck religiously to a four-hour routine organised by Father who wrote meticulously in my Baby Book about every little event from my first hiccup to my graduation to the potty. A new book by Dr. Spock was the most popular baby book of the day and my parents stuck rigidly to the advice given regards routine and everything else. Mum recalled how she would have to endure my screams and howls of hunger whilst pacing up and down the living room waiting for the clock to show the correct feeding time. Unbelievable these days. Yet somehow, I survived, and I was adored by both of them.

Home from hospital at two weeks old, Dad holds me for the first time

My parents could not have been more different. Mother was extrovert, easy going, affectionate, humorous, and optimistic; father was introvert, serious, reserved, orderly, and pessimistic. They met in 1940, just before the horrific blitz on Liverpool, when my father's ship, HMS Vanoc, was in dock. At this time, he was Acting Petty Officer Telegraphist and had risen through the ranks from a lowly sailor, scrubbing decks. Walter Percy Edney, was twenty-two years old and had come from a working-class family in Bognor Regis. Carefully counting the pennies was normal for them although they had never known hunger, nor ever been poorly clothed. He was not without determination and perseverance, which is what led him to eventually become an officer of the Royal Navy - serving with bravery and fortitude through World War II.

It is still a mystery to me how he managed to educate himself and pass all his exams thus rising to become an officer.

Walter joined the navy in 1933 as a fifteen-year-old sailor, determined to do more than just scrub the decks for the rest of his life.

He had left behind an ailing father who had worked down the mines and suffered chronic lung problems, and a sickly mother. Both were pretty much illiterate and did not encourage education in any shape or form. His brother, Bernard, had left school and was working in manual labour. My father was different. Wanting to make something of himself, he signed up for the navy, imagining himself as one day being the captain. giving the orders

How he loved to give orders! He would not suffer fools gladly and everyone was expected to do their duty. It served him well. In order for him to rise to the next step of his career he needed to pass exams of course. His education was far too inadequate. So, with the help of some private tuition, he waited until he was eighteen, signed up for twelve years, was seconded to HMS Vincent, and then took an exam to become a wireless telegraphist. HMS Iron Duke was his next assignment, and shortly after that he was transferred to HMS Nelson, the flagship of the Home Fleet. After his transfer to HMS Maidstone two years later he passed the exam to become a Trained Operator. As War broke in 1939 Walter had managed to pass another exam to become Leading Telegraphist in charge of ship's communications on HMS Vanoc, the ship that would take him through the Battle of the Atlantic, and beyond. The details of his experiences through all this terrible conflict can be read in his book Scuppers to Skipper, available in bookshops and online.

Walter, 1951

By the time I was born Walter had become a petty officer – indeed the youngest petty office ever to serve in the Royal Navy. He later told me that he found socialising with other officers on the ship quite difficult as, unlike him, they had been to Public Schools, university, and Dartmoor College. Somehow my father managed the social graces and conversation to make life long acquaintances and friends and to be admired by so many. He was mentioned in Despatches twice for his bravery and courage.

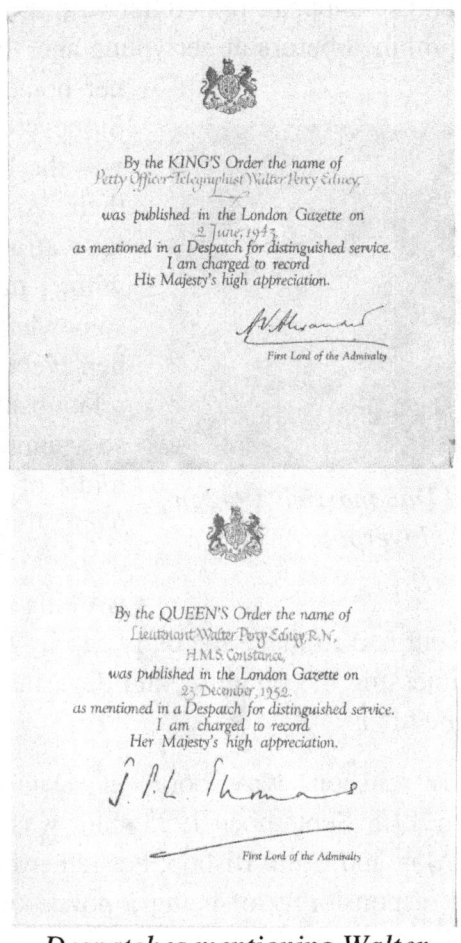

> By the KING'S Order the name of
> Petty Officer Telegraphist Walter Percy Sidney
> was published in the London Gazette on
> 2 June, 1943
> as mentioned in a Despatch for distinguished service.
> I am charged to record
> His Majesty's high appreciation.
>
> *First Lord of the Admiralty*

> By the QUEEN'S Order the name of
> Lieutenant Walter Percy Sidney, R.N.,
> H.M.S. Constance,
> was published in the London Gazette on
> 23 December, 1952.
> as mentioned in a Despatch for distinguished service.
> I am charged to record
> Her Majesty's high appreciation.
>
> *First Lord of the Admiralty*

Despatches mentioning Walter

In his autobiography, which he wrote a few years before his death, he writes, "The most momentous event of my life happened on Monday, 10th November, 1940" when he describes how he went ashore with his friend Jack Oldfield for a meal and drinks, meeting up with several other ship mates who were planning an encounter with girls they had met at a dance previously. My mother was one of those girls, she was just seventeen. "I found Thelma very lively, very entertaining, most attractive with a tremendous personality and sex appeal. I plied her with drink, in which she had not imbibed before at her young age, then escorted her home by tram to Stoneycroft". This was the beginning of their sixty-two-year love affair. To begin with, mother was somewhat apprehensive about the relationship. She was so young and, in the midst of war, people were living by the day. She was working as an accountant, and had to make the daily trip by bus to work, regularly witnessing the bombing and devastation reigning over her home town.

Mum and Dad married 1942 in Liverpool

Thelma May Bishop was born in Davidson Road, Liverpool on 13th September 1923. She was the second daughter of May and Ernie Bishop; her father having taken the role and responsibility of being a police officer at the end of the First World War. This position came with a terraced house, for which they were extremely grateful in these times of dire poverty. May had qualified as a seamstress, so between them they were making enough money to live fairly comfortably. Thelma's younger sister, Mavis, was born nine years later after they had moved to 41 Anstey Road in Old Swan. This was a three-bed end of terrace house – with an indoor bathroom! Thelma loved her little sister and was horrified when plans were made to have younger children evacuated at the beginning of the war. Mavis was highly sensitive and refused to go. An air raid shelter was built in their little garden, where they could safely hide until the sirens gave the 'all clear'.

May 1941. The Blitz on Liverpool had begun, causing fear and destruction to the whole city. One particular night was a night that would change their lives forever. Grandad Ernie was on duty in the town. Iris, Mum's eldest sister, was in town at the cinema with friends. Nana May was at home with nine-year-old Mavis when the sirens started. They went down into the air raid shelter as usual. Some short time later nana told Mavis she needed to go into the house for something. She was only gone a minute when a bomb fell on Anstey Road, demolishing half the houses. Although their house had not been hit, the tremor and shock of the bomb made the doors and windows in the house lock tight. Nana May could not get out. Mavis lay there all night presuming her mother was dead. The next morning nana found Mavis in a shocking nervous state. She never recovered. By the time she was a teenager she was unable to function normally, so doctors advised a lobotomy. As we know now, this was a terrible treatment that left the patient lacking memory and unable to relate to others appropriately. As for Iris, she had run with friends to a nearby underground air raid shelter, where she said, "it was crowded with so many people I couldn't breathe. People were smoking. I had to get out!". So, after running like a mad hare, bombs dropping all around her, she cowered in a field near her house until eventually, she made it back to Anstey Road. The following day she learned that a bomb had made a direct hit on the air raid shelter and killed everyone, including her best friends. Yet another example of how fate played its part in our lives.

Mother, meanwhile, was making her way back from Bognor by train, having met her future in-laws for the first time, completely unaware of what had happened in Liverpool. As she got off the train her heart broke.

In her words, "I tumbled off the train in dismay, stepped over the debris, I thought I was having a nightmare. There was an eerie silence everywhere. I had no choice but to walk the five miles, stepping over broken buildings, broken people, broken spirits, terrified what I would find when I reached Anstey Road. Would my house still be there, and would my family still be alive?". She was relieved to find them all safe, but their lives would never be the same.

When the war ended there were street parties and dancing all over Liverpool and of course the rest of the country. Yet there was one more incident that would haunt my mother for the rest of her life. When it was announced that war prisoners would be returning to Liverpool docks, the people were invited to come and welcome them home. Mum couldn't wait. She stood there among hundreds of other people, waiting to cheer and wave flags for these poor survivors. As the survivors from Japan came down the gang planks, waving their arms in relief to be home, the crowd turned pale and silent. Mum was horrified to see nothing more than bruised skeletons coming towards them. She shivered in horror as she wondered how any human being could treat another one in this way. When she also learned of the atrocities they inflicted on our poor captured sons, too horrific to be described in this memoir, she never forgave the Japanese for the rest of her life. Yet the spirit of the Liverpool people rose above it all and communities came together to support one another in a way that has made Liverpool the unique and welcoming place that it still is today.

MY EARLY YEARS

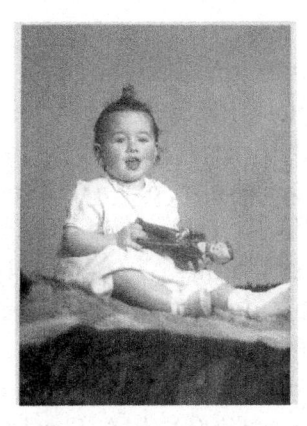

The earliest memory I have is of being on a beach in Wallasey, slowly sinking into slimy sinking sand and thinking I would drown. I was four years old. Fortunately, an older friend managed to pull me out and I ran home to tell my horrified mother the whole terrifying story. Unlike today, it was normal for young children to run off and play, unsupervised, within the locality. My father was away fighting the Korean War, and my mother had considered me mature and confident enough to go off with my little friends by myself.

By 1949, Dad had been promoted to Lieutenant on HMS Zodiac, stationed in Portland, Dorset. A small terraced house was found nearby in Weymouth. Fortunately for us, finances were not too much of a problem. Dad was earning good money in the Royal Navy. I always remember travelling first class on the trains. For many others in the

In the garden of our first bungalow in Gordon Road, Emsworth. 1948

country, however, things were vastly different. Poverty was widespread, and children malnourished. Orphanages were full.

I was 21 months old when my new baby sister arrived; Julia Annette. Mum adored babies and I think I was expected to 'grow up' quite quickly once Julia was on the scene. Julia was fair skinned and had a more placid nature, not like me who had a very low tolerance threshold if I did not reach my intended goal or expectations. After a lovely summer playing on the beach most days, Mum and Dad decided it was time to buy a small place of their own. A little bungalow between Southbourne and Emsworth - not far from Chichester - that cost them £2000. 14A Gordon Road.

It became obvious a car was needed for the regular journey to Portsmouth so a 1934 Morris was purchased – it had no boot and a top speed of 40MPH.

Next door to our house was a monkey tied up in the garden. I have absolutely no notion how it came to be there. One morning whilst I was playing in the garden the monkey managed to escape from its leash. It jumped over the fence and came hurtling towards me, very aggressively! I was terrified. Mum immediately came to the rescue, snatching me away just in the 'nick of time'. She lost her temper with the neighbours over this incident and I don't know what happened to the poor thing after that.

Our life in Emsworth was happy and carefree to a large extent. Mum was so devoted to us, her children, she spent her days happily wandering around the quay in the village, letting us feed the ducks and look at the boats bobbing up and down, the fish being hauled in by the nets, and the old mill churning away. She would chat to the shopkeepers and anyone who happened to be standing nearby.

Happy and carefree

Some days she would walk a mile to a local allotment to buy fresh vegetables from the farmer and although her repertoire of food was not exactly varied and extensive, she always put a good dinner on the plate with a delicious pudding to follow. Our favourite was roast meat and vegetables, followed by lemon meringue pie or treacle pudding. She made biscuits and cakes herself and, by the time I was nine years old I was making the cakes for the family myself.

The family in 1950

I was two and a half when Dad was informed of his next appointment. Joining HMS Constance, he was told he would be departing for Hong Kong very soon and he knew he would be gone for two and a half years. Arrangements were to be made for Mum, me, and Julia to join Dad later. In the meantime, Mum decided she would rather be nearer her family in Liverpool and chose a flat in Wallasey across the water, 31 Caithness Drive, would be quieter and more pleasant.

Whilst we were to be away, the bungalow in Emsworth was to be rented out. We lived in our temporary residence, a large flat by the river in Wallasey, waiting for the trip with trepidation. However, the Korean War broke out and all plans for families to travel to Hong Kong were abandoned. No-one had any idea how long the war might last. We had no idea that Dad would not be returning for nearly three years. Julia was only 6 months old when he left, and I had grown into a confident two-year-old. I began Sunday

School, aged three, and had been walking to church by myself since I started. It was within sight of our front window and Mum used to watch me walk there and back.

Of course we all missed Dad so much and were only able to communicate with occasional letters. I still have some of the cards and drawings that Mum encouraged me to send him. We were always so thrilled when a letter arrived from him, although sadly these letters no longer survive.

1950

The day came when Mum received notification that Dad would be returning home. We immediately packed up and returned to Emsworth. The day he arrived at the train station was memorable for all of us.

Dad writes: *"Thelma, Christine, and Julia were waiting for me on the platform. It is impossible to describe a reunion such as this after such a long time. Christine could well remember me but to Julia I was just some man coming to intrude on their happy little lives."*

I can imagine my excitement as we stood on the platform waiting for the train to arrive, all dressed in our best coats and shoes. We were always immaculately dressed, and Mum would never accept second-hand clothes, or food for that matter. Our family were reunited at last but very soon we would be leaving Emsworth, travelling eight hundred miles north.

After an extensive leave, Dad eventually received his next appointment. He was to take command of a motor minesweeper in Scotland, operating in the Firth of Forth and based near Rosyth. This was to be a two-year appointment, in command of a small crew of around twenty men and one other 1st Lieutenant. Their job was to sail out on exercises to pinpoint mines using sonar transmission and, if found, to detonate them. Dad admits that he found the exercises necessary but laborious; at least he was able to come home to sleep at night. To begin with we were settled in a first floor flat of a large house facing the Firth of Forth in Burntisland. Once again our bungalow in Emsworth was rented out. Mum found herself pregnant again and the time had come for me to start school. My first

Expecting the next family member

day at school happened to be my birthday. I had been looking forward to going and on the first morning all the parents were there to help settle the children into their new classroom.

Mum was fussing around me, like all the other Mums and Dads. "Will you be all right darling?"

"Yes, I will," I replied. "And you can go now - you don't need to fuss". My first sign of independence had loomed!

When Mum came to meet me at the end of the day she was horrified to see that I had a big gash across my forehead. Apparently, a child had thrown a stone during the lunchtime break and it hit me straight in the face!

Education in Scotland was taken very seriously; teachers were extremely strict and discipline harsh. From the first day we were ordered to sit behind our desks, arms folded and no speaking. We were all terrified! Formal lessons began straight away; homework was assigned as a page of reading every night. If we did not learn this page of reading by the next day, we were punished. Fortunately, I was lucky in that my mother, with great patience, would sit with me every night whilst I learned the words.

I can still remember the morning that Teacher said we were going to be tested on our counting skills.

"You will write the numbers 1 to 100 and the first one to finish will raise their hand," Teacher commanded in her very strict tone. I was determined to be first to finish and I scribbled furiously on the page, raising my arm as soon as I had written "100". I felt very proud as Teacher declared, "Christine is the winner. Come forward and receive the prize." I was so excited to receive a bar of chocolate!

As a youngster I was very conscientious and aimed for 100% success in everything I did. I believe this was partly the genes I had inherited from my father, and partly the way my parents always complimented me on everything that I endeavoured to achieve.

There was never a time when I felt a failure, only a need to try harder next time.

A few weeks later an event occurred that I will never forget. Julia, only three and half, had become ill with flu and was bedridden.

"I'm calling the Doctor," said Mum, extremely concerned.

"No, No, No! Don't want the Doctor, don't want the Doctor!" yelled Julia, screaming.

Another day went by, and another. Eventually, Julia became worse and, much to Julia's dismay, the Doctor was called. "She's got pneumonia and needs to be rushed to hospital immediately," the Doctor announced. It sounded like a life and death situation.

We all went together in the ambulance and were subsequently informed that she was seriously ill with double pneumonia and may have died that night. Julia was hysterical when Mum had to leave her there and go home, which were the rules in those days. How cruel! We tried to visit the next day but were told it was not in the best interest of the sick child to be visited by relatives. She would be allowed one hour on a Wednesday and two hours on a Sunday. I remember looking through the window trying to see her lying in the bed. Mum was heartbroken. She tried over and over again to get in there to see her sick daughter but was refused. Julia was in that hospital for six weeks and during that time she had cried herself into a frenzy and must have felt totally abandoned.

August of that year brought joy and sadness within days of each. I was six years old and looking forward to the arrival of my new baby sister or brother when Dad received a letter to say his mother was seriously ill and wasn't expected to live long. She had been diagnosed with cancer and, unable to swallow, had been admitted to hospital where she died very soon afterwards. She was in her mid fifties. The only photograph I have of her with me was taken when I was about three months old. Born in to family of labourers near Amberley, Sussex, Dora a had had a life of drudgery and stress. They had lived in poverty and for most of her adult life she had been unwell, trying to bring up two boys, and a husband who was working at the gas works for long hours. I was told she kept chickens that they used to kill and eat on a Sunday and Grandfather Percy grew all his own vegetables in their tiny back garden.

They would wait for the horse and cart to go by and then pick up the horse poo as compost for the allotment.

Christine with Grandma & Grandad, Bognor, May 1948

By the early 1950's Grandfather had retired on sick pay. His hacking cough, caused by damage to his lungs from his job had left him almost incapacitated. Compensation was unheard of in those days. He had worked six days a week, shovelling coal into a furnace from which gas was extracted as it burned. This was then taken from the furnace and sprayed with water to produce coke. It was hard, hot, and dirty work. He would return as black as a coal miner and would have to bathe in a tin bath.

Dad had not been an easy boy to bring up with his fierce independence, stubbornness, and intolerance, yet it was these qualities that saw him through his naval career and the war years. *"I was self-willed, stubborn, and disobedient"*, Dad writes in his autobiography: *"My mother suffered with chronic asthma most of her life and trying to deal with me led her to threaten me being sent to the Lavant Home for delinquent children near Midhurst or that a policeman was coming to take me away. I would stand by the window looking out for the policeman whilst assuring*

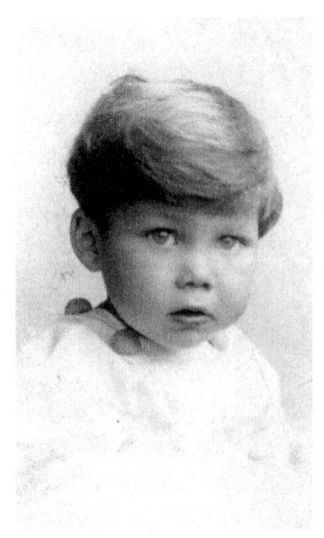

Walter aged 18months   *Aged 9 with brother Bern*

mother that I would behave in future."

Mum told me that her mother-in-law did not approve of her as a suitable wife for her darling boy because she was "too flighty" and "liked to stay up late in the evening playing games and such like". There were no games in the Edney household, life was about survival, bed at 8pm and up at 5am to start work! After Dad died, I studied his autobiography in more detail. I realised that Percy Edney was probably not his real father at all. But that is another story.

My sister, Karen, arrived on 10th August 1953. She was blond with blue eyes, and I was thrilled to have a new baby sister! I had been pushing a doll around in my dolls pram for years; it was so wonderful to have a proper baby to push. All my friends were very envious. After having two daughters, Mum had secretly been wanting a baby boy but none of us knew that at the time.

I quickly became a 'second Mum' to Karen, taking her across to the park for walks, looking at the ducks on the pond, and pushing her on the swings.

With new sister Karen

We had by now moved out of the flat and into a small, pretty bungalow, opposite a beautiful park in Kirkcaldy. I would set off for school at 8.30am on my own and walk down to catch the school bus, doing the same on the return home journey in the afternoon. I felt very independent and confident, and Mum was always complimentary about my ability to cope with things by myself.

As it was the year of the Queen's Coronation we were told we would be running for the Queen at our sports day. I was never very good at sports, nor running, but I did my best and we were all awarded with a small coronation tin of little chocolates. I still have that tin to this day.

Meanwhile, Dad would be taking a break from the minesweeping job. The ship was being replaced by HMS Aveley which would be fitted with all the latest

H.M.S. Aveley

minesweeping equipment in Cowes on the Isle of Wight. Dad was expected to supervise the completion and accept the ship on behalf of the Admiralty. After a spell in Portsmouth, Dad and the ship made its way to Scotland to resume minesweeping duties. Several months later he was informed that the Duke of Edinburgh may need the assistance of HMS Aveley to transport him to Dunfermline across the Firth of Forth, should the weather be unsuitable for Naval Launch. This was indeed the case and, at the appointed hour, Dad writes: *"the jetty was alive with Captains, Commanders and others, my gangway ready with the piping party and myself at the head to greet him on*

Whitby. Dad (on the left) Commander, Sub-Lieutenant, and dignitaries.

board. I took him up to the Bridge, immediately letting go and sailing. We had a pleasant journey across, chatting about various naval matters. I had to wait for him to return to bring him back again. Later, Dad received from the Duke a signed photograph of himself which was hung in their wardroom."

By the end of 1955, our spell in Scotland was over. Dad had received his next appointment as barrack guard officer at RN Barracks in Chatham. He was not exactly excited about this new posting as this was the first time he would not be on a ship at sea, one of the reasons he joined up for the Navy! Once again, Mum had to start packing up our things and I prepared to leave my primary school, along with all my friends for a new adventure.

During the summer of that year we had a special visitor for a week. It was my Great Auntie Beth, my mother's auntie on her father's side. Beth Bishop had been born in Cheshire in 1888 to my great-grandparents - Ernest and Elizabeth.

Beth was their first child. Within a short time, it was noticed that she was not developing normally, and it was soon realised that she suffered from dwarfism. It must have been horrific for Ernest and Elizabeth as there was not much support in those days. In fact, circuses would use such people as 'freaks' for their shows. Elizabeth gave birth to two more children within four years, but she was unable to cope. She turned to alcohol. She had to have spells in institutions to help 'cure' her, and her two boys were regularly farmed out to relatives. The only option was to have Beth admitted to a crippleage, a cruel environment, especially for a sensitive child like Beth. The whole family offered support, my grandfather Ernie had become very fond of her. A place was found in London. John Groom's Crippleage and Flower Girls Mission it was called. Not exactly near to Liverpool! I don't think she had any visitors, just letters and cards. In fact, I have in my possession a card sent to her from my grandfather in 1914, dressed in his army uniform, when he was about to set off with the army for the First World War. Mother would always try to get her out whenever possible and bring her to our house for a holiday. We were always told she was "very special". She so enjoyed her time with us and we spoilt her rotten. In the 1950's, mother managed to get her out of the London crippleage and move her nearer to us so we could visit her often. She told Mum she had not been treated kindly there over the years, which upset Mum greatly. An article that appeared in The Guardian in 2007 described the words of an 'inmate' in this place who said:

"The women were expected to do all their own washing by hand, as well as their ironing and keeping their individual cubicles clean. The cubicle was like a horse box. We had a bed, which was attached to the wall, a wardrobe, a

dressing table, one chair, and curtains where a door should be. There was no privacy. And when we were in the factory you had to keep your eyes on the table and work. If you didn't, you'd end up with a poke in the back."

The last time we saw her in the care home was just before she died in 1961. She slipped her watch off her wrist and handed it to me saying "I want you to have this, Christine." I was so astonished that she chose me to have it. I have looked after it all this time and it is now stored carefully in a box with my other "special things".

Me, Julia, Karen and Auntie Beth, 1955

BACK TO EMSWORTH

After having moved back to our bungalow in Emsworth, Julia and I were sent to the nearest primary school in Southbourne. My classroom was in a pre-fab hut in the playground. Before I could settle in, I was told I would be moved up two classes because my academic ability was far higher than a normal seven-year-old. I was mortified having to sit with nine-year-olds where I felt completely out of my depth. Mum and Dad were delighted that their eldest daughter was so advanced. I was not! The Scottish education ensured that children were always ahead. I'm not sure if that applies now but it certainly did in those days. Nevertheless, I quickly made friends. One was a girl called Rosemary, who lived in my road. We would share my sweets and read Bunty magazines together. I would call on her to come and play with me down by the stream or go cycling across the meadows at weekends. Sometimes we would head off towards Bosham and run across the waterlogged fields to play around rusty old abandoned boats. Yes, we were only seven years old! Children were given complete freedom in those days.

"Come back in time for lunch," Mum would call as I scooted off down the road. I would often be sent into Emsworth for a bit of shopping for Mum about half a mile away. My treat was to stop off at the cake shop on the way to town and buy a jam puff. How I enjoyed that when I got home!

It was a happy time for us. Mum found herself pregnant again and we duly found a larger house at the top of the road. A large semi-detached house called Greenways. It looked huge compared to our little bungalow! It had four bedrooms and two large sitting rooms. I can still picture the inside of the house. A large front sitting room, a smaller

"Greenways"

back dining room with a hatch through to the kitchen. Going upstairs there was a little door in the wall which led into the loft. I recall going in there and being shocked to find a gas mask from the Second World War, thrown in amongst all the boxes and bags that had been brought with us. I couldn't wait to try it on. The other children wanted to have a go too, so we took it in turns to strap it around our face. I remember being unable to breath and wondering how on earth people could have worn those things. Fortunately there had never been an occasion to use it.

Every morning I would cross the road to catch the bus to school by myself, then walk home in the afternoon, a distance of just over a mile, having often spent my bus money on sweets. I used to envy my friends whose mother was always standing at the school gate. On the odd occasion Mum would come to meet me pushing Karen in the pram. How wonderful it was to see Mum standing waiting for me! As for Julia she was transferred to a private school nearby, the thought being that she would benefit from more individual attention. So, with Mum's busy life, I had to look after myself. I can remember one day we had a story competition. We were encouraged to write a story and were told the winner would receive a present. I can't remember what I wrote about, but I do remember holding my breath as the teacher announced the winner. "Well done, Christine Edney, you have won the prize for the best story this term." I was shocked! I think the present consisted of some chocolates and my story was read out to the rest of the class. I felt very proud. I used to love writing little stories. Mum would find them on bits of paper around the house.

Our little back garden was the place where we could create our own world. Digging holes in the garden ("let's dig down to Australia!"), watching the butterflies, pushing each other on the swing, playing games and trying to keep Karen amused. She was not an easy toddler. I think jealousy of her baby brother was mostly to blame, but she would cry and scream for the slightest thing. She started getting mouth ulcers because she wasn't eating food put in front of her. All attention-seeking behaviours. I took her under my wing and gave her much of the attention she craved. Mum was often out shopping and left me in charge, so I learned to become very responsible at a young age.

"There is one thing you need to know" said Mum one afternoon whilst we were shopping in town. "If ever you see a black person you must not stare, is that understood?" I don't remember seeing a black person in our village, but we were told that foreigners were arriving all the time and we 'needed to be prepared'. Rock and roll had arrived. Elvis Presley was top of the bill, not that I was a big fan, but it was normal to hear people singing his songs around the neighbourhood. "One o'clock, two o'clock, three o'clock, rock!" Bill Haley's voice would ring out. It was a new era and the vinyl records started flying off the shelves. We had a few records ourselves but not Elvis, if I remember rightly. Mum and Dad preferred music from the musicals, or Dean Martin. They had brought back from New York the entire vinyl collection from Oklahoma having seen it on Broadway. They carried those records around with them from house to house, country to country, all their lives. I now have them stored safely in my garage somewhere. Britain was slowly recovering from the war, there was less doom and gloom around and dire poverty would soon be a thing of the past. Mum talked about incidents that happened in the war so many times, I used to wonder why she was still affected by something that happened so long ago. Of course, anything that happens before you are born is 'so long ago', but for them, it had only finished three years before I was born. Dad never talked about it.

Meanwhile at Chatham Docks, Dad was having to suffer a job he disliked intensely. His duties included having complete responsibility for security; responsibility for the discipline of all ratings in the Barracks; to train 100 men for ceremonial duties; and the weekly divisional parade every Friday. His long hours meant he could not return home in the evenings, so we only saw him at weekends. I remember sitting on the garden wall in the front of the house on Friday afternoons, waiting for him to come home.

"Here he comes now!" I would shout to the other children.

He always brought us sweets, then he would come into the house. Soon after greeting Mum and getting changed, he would put his hands on his hips and say in a strong voice, "So what's all this mess then? I can't sit down until it's all cleared away."

He had been in Barracks all week where everything was 'ship shape' and then he returns to a house that looked like Bedlam. Mum never minded if we left all our belongings, toys and clothes all over the place. We often had sheets draped across the furniture to make dens. Sometimes the weekends were a bit tense; Mum enjoyed her carefree life with us, but Dad wanted everything 'in order'.

On occasional Sundays we would all pile in the car and head off to Bognor to visit Dad's brother, Bern, his wife, Sheila, and their two boys, Kevin, and Roger. They lived in the same little terraced house that had been rented by my grandfather all his life. Percy would sit in the corner, grunting occasionally, not making conversation with any of

*Top row: left to right:
Kevin, Dad, Auntie Sheila, Grandad, Mum.
Bottom row: Jonathan, Julia, Me, Karen, Roger*

us. Bern and Sheila would chat about their everyday life, present us with a big tea, and enjoy our company. I was always astonished how they managed to live with a toilet in a shed at the bottom of the garden. How I hated using it! Soon after these visits, poor Sheila was diagnosed with a tumour. She was pregnant with her third child and desperately wanted a little girl. She died unaware that the baby she had been carrying was her little girl. It was a very sad time for us. Mum was particularly fond of her. Kevin and Roger were only aged five or six at the time. The shocking thing for Mum was that Bern was dating someone else within weeks of Sheila's death and they married soon after. It would appear Freda had been 'waiting on the sidelines' for Bern and pounced on him as soon as Sheila died. Freda treated Grandfather Percy badly and was short tempered with the boys. Mum could not bear to set eyes on her. We stopped visiting but Kevin and Roger would stay with us in the holidays whenever they liked.

My little brother Jonathan arrived on 7th April, 1955. The joy of now having a son! Mum wanted to tell the world about it. She'd been wanting a boy ever since I was born, and now she had one. I was thrilled as well, yet little did I know that Mum had almost died giving birth to him. Whilst she was in hospital, nana had come down to look after us. Apparently, Mum had given birth naturally without any problems, but then when the afterbirth was being delivered, she started losing a lot of blood. She lost consciousness and, she says, she remembers the doctor saying, "I think we've lost her."

She knew she was dying! Miraculously, however, she came around. Two weeks later she returned home. My sister Karen had forgotten her mother and clung to nana. I became the 'second Mum', looking after Karen when necessary and, over time, becoming a second Mum to Jonathan as well. I adored both of them.

Some days Mum would take us on the bus to Chichester to buy new clothes. She would always remind us of the fact that in the 1850's my great-great-grandfather, Charles

Family Complete

Bishop, sang in the cathedral and was well known throughout the district.

"There's the cathedral where he sang," she would proudly point out. "He had a wonderful voice and was loved by many people." Fifty-six years later, his story would be told on BBC TV and broadcast to over 60 million people. Pity Mum was no longer alive to see it. More on that later.

At weekends we would often go to Arundel Castle. It was a favourite of mother's. Dad would rather stay at home at weekends and just potter, but Mum needed to take us all out somewhere and she enjoyed the opportunity to do so. She loved the gardens particularly, and over the years she would visit many gardens in various parts of the country. In the summer months, we would head off to the coast and swim. Very occasionally Mum would suggest a day trip to the funfair in Southsea when we lived in the south, and New Brighton when we went up north.

"Who's coming with me on the big wheel?" I would shout. We all loved the rides; the faster and higher the better as far as I was concerned.

On Sundays we would have a quiet day. We were told it was not appropriate to have fun on Sundays. "You're not going out to play with friends on a Sunday. Nor are we going to the cinema because it's closed." So, we would amuse ourselves indoors; get games out, play Scrabble, make, and eat good food, and go for a family walk in the afternoon. I loved nothing better than doing a crossword with Dad or playing a game that involved strategy and discovery. These games were too serious for Mum, she preferred activities that involved lots of laughter and cheating! She took nothing seriously. I read a lot of books, too, and around this time I started enjoying Enid Blyton's Famous Five, and her Secret Seven books.

In order to get our pocket money, we had to tidy up our bedroom on a Saturday morning, which became the routine and was never missed. I liked to spend my pocket money on comics and sweets, then save a little for presents for the family. Dad always maintained that youngsters should earn every penny they got, and he stuck to that belief all during our growing up years.

Once Mum said, "Christine, why don't you start going to Brownies? There's a local group you can go to." But it wasn't my thing. Why on earth would I want to dress up in a brown uniform every week and go marching around, doing things by order? No, that definitely wasn't for me! I preferred to be a free spirit and organise others! That was my nature and it still is to this day.

During our time at Greenways, with four children and an absent husband, Mum, deciding she needed some help in the house, employed a local lady, a Mrs Lawson, who soon became a familiar part of our household. I think she came up three mornings per week. Mum regarded her as a good friend and would often chat with her over a cup of tea. A few months later, Mum was somewhat disconcerted to find that money was regularly going missing. She started to make a note of the numbers in an attempt to discover the mystery. Other items had gone missing as well. Eventually, she began to suspect Mrs Lawson. She did not want to believe that someone she regarded as a friend could possibly be stealing from her. One day she set up a trap. She took a note of the numbers on the pound notes. After they had disappeared she confronted Mrs Lawson.

"Me?" Mrs Lawson looked horrified. "Of course I wouldn't take anything of yours." She was in tears. Mum felt she should report it to the Police and after extensive search, many items, including the money, were found hidden in her garage. Even items of clothing. She was fined and prosecuted. It left Mum with an overwhelming distrust of people from that day on.

One of my greatest joys and my greatest sadness happened during the next few months. My eighth birthday was approaching, and I'd been asked what I wanted for my birthday. "I'd love a puppy!" I declared, not ever imagining in my wildest dreams that I would get one. But, yes, on the morning of my birthday, Mum walked in carrying a little bundle wrapped in a warm cloth. I was so surprised and excited. This little puppy was showered with so much love and affection. Yet my joy was not to last. A short time after he came into our home, he appeared to be ill. Not eating nor responding. We took him to the vet who confirmed he had the dreaded disease, distemper! I was completely mortified. Nothing could be done, and the poor little thing passed away a few days later. It took me a long time to recover from this awful experience.

Every week without fail I would write a letter to my grandmother. As she was partly deaf we could not speak to her on the phone. She must have appreciated and kept my letters because I have a couple of them in my possession now. When the school holidays came around, I always asked if I could go to Liverpool to stay with her and my papa.

I loved being there and seeing all my cousins, aunts, and uncles. I would be put on a train, by myself, with food and drinks, my embroidery or knitting, and books to read, and I would make the long journey to Liverpool Lime Street. I think it took about eight hours to get there in those days. My nana would be waiting at the station for me, and I would eagerly jump off the train and we'd head off to catch a bus to Anstey Road. Having her all to myself was a privilege.

I was so used to being part of a large family where 'the little ones' always came first, and I had many duties to perform. At my grandparent's home in Liverpool, it was heaven to be able to do what I liked and get so much personal attention! Very often, papa was not well and stayed home, so nana would take me to town and treat me to afternoon tea in an exclusive restaurant in somewhere like Lewis's or Owen Owen. She would buy me treats and then we'd visit my cousins for dinner. Sometimes I would be left there to stay overnight with them, which was a great treat. As nana was considerably deaf in both ears, it became normal to always have to shout so she could hear me. She had lost most of her hearing when she was a young girl and had suffered Scarlet Fever. Yet she always had a positive approach to life. She wore a hearing aid and once said, "It comes in very handy to be deaf when you get fed up with someone talking incessantly – I just dislodge my hearing aid so I can't hear them!" She had a book on her bookshelf called, Positive Living, and I always liked to look at that book whenever I stayed there. She would get down the big box of old photographs and I would pour over them, asking who all the relatives were. After nana died I often wondered what happened to that box. All my relatives deny ever seeing it. Mum in particular was upset that the box disappeared.

"Nana"

Nana was very regal. She loved lacy embroidered tablecloths, invariably made by herself. She would shop in the best shops and drink tea in the most expensive tea rooms. The little house in Anstey Road had a tiny garden where they had lived since 1926 when my mother was three years old. The story goes that my nana wanted to live in a more middle-class area, over on the Wirral. She had her heart set on buying a house there. Houses were being offered at very low prices and a deposit of only £5 would secure it. However, papa was nervous about investing in such a huge commitment and after much consideration decided they should 'play safe' and rent the terraced house in Liverpool. Nana was disappointed and tried to make the best of it but I think in later years they realised that had been a big mistake.

Nana was refined, there is no doubt. She was a wonderful tailoress and made clothes for all the family. An avid churchgoer, she would relate interesting tales of the folk at the church and took an active role in helping others less fortunate than herself. She regarded herself as a friend of the minister – Rev. Beaman, who would often call on her for a cup of tea.

She used to tell me that she was the great-great granddaughter of the illegitimate son of a baron from Lancashire. As a child growing up I learned that this Baron, Lord Skelmersdale, had an illegitimate son, James, in 1811. He was christened on the estate of Lathom House and was later adopted to a certain Martha Battersby. James Battersby became a rope maker and moved to Liverpool where he married and had several children, including Thomas, born in 1864. Thomas married a Protestant Irish girl, Mary Pollock, and their eldest daughter was Sarah, (my nana's mother). Sarah was able to leave school at ten-years-old, due to being highly intelligent. This story was passed by word of mouth through the family although we have no documented evidence. Nana and her mother, Sarah were so sophisticated and intelligent, and all carried the genes of longevity, living well into their nineties. She did not mix with the neighbours in the road, who appeared, her opinion, 'course and common'. Only her next-door neighbour, Mrs Bibby, was her friend. Mum had never been allowed to play in the road with the neighbour's children, and I was also forbidden. I was also told that you didn't mix with Catholics. The story went that Liverpool, apparently, was ruined by the Irish coming over in their droves during the potato famine and after. They took over everyone's jobs and stole and pilfered anything they could lay their hands on. There was a real division between Protestants and Catholics. I was not allowed to go anywhere in the Catholic area, such as the Docks. Mum told me the Catholic children threw stones at her and her friends on their way to school in the mornings. I was shocked by the poverty in Liverpool, and the grime and dirt. It always seemed so very cold and wet. The number of stray dogs and cats running around was appalling. Such a contrast from our home in the south!

I was eight and a half when I learned our time in Emsworth was over. I would have to say goodbye to my classmates and friends. Dad was leaving Chatham Barracks for a posting in Malta

Our last formal photo before departing for Malta.

MALTA

Lieutenant Commander Walter Edney was now in command of HMS Fenton, a minesweeper belonging to a squadron in the Mediterranean. Trouble had flared up in Cyprus between the Turks and the Cypriots. Turkey claimed Cyprus to be theirs. Greece also claimed the island, but it was, as far as we were concerned, British. Arms were being smuggled into the island from both Greece and Turkey, and if the fighting was to be contained it was necessary to prevent such arms from getting through. HMS Fenton was one of the minesweepers engaged in patrol. Dad was eager to begin his new assignment, but first he had to work out arrangements for the family to join him on the island. He was told he would have to take up his appointment first, find accommodation for us, and then get permission from the Admiralty. Consequently, we let our house out and went to Liverpool to stay with my grandparents for a few weeks before Dad left for Malta. There we waited for news of our accommodation arrangements.

Eventually we were told that a large flat had been found in Sliema for us, and we had been allocated a passage by air. Dad knew he would be away when we arrived, so he had arranged for a friend to meet us at the airport. I can still remember the horrors of that flight. Having travelled by train to London first class with all our luggage, we stayed in a comfortable hotel overnight. The next day we arrived at the airport and boarded this small lightweight plane where we were squashed into seats. The plane would be landing in Nice to refuel. We were all excited, but scared. The air pressure in those days made flying very uncomfortable and we all experienced an agonising ear ache, both on the upward and downward flights. Jonathan and Karen were screaming in pain. The only thing that made the journey less traumatic was the arrival of a little tray of food, all set out in different compartments and very palatable, I thought.

After our arrival at Luga airport, Malta, Mum, with four children in tow, looked around for this friend of Dad who was supposed to meet us and take us to our accommodation. Worryingly, he was not there, no one could speak English, and she didn't know what to do. It was hot, and the little ones were crying. Not a good start! Eventually she found a telephone and somehow found the number of a relevant person. They sent a taxi and we were dropped off at a flat on the third floor. I still have a memory of running into the flat and seeing a refrigerator for the first time. But it wasn't working, nobody had switched it on. There was no water to drink, all water had to be boiled before consuming. This was just the start. We went up to the bedrooms, all exhausted, dripping with perspiration, only to find that the beds were riddled with bed bugs! My poor mother, left alone with us all in these horrible conditions. We slept on the floor that first night. Mum did not hesitate to contact someone the following morning. In fact, she 'kicked up merry hell'.

We were immediately moved to another apartment nearby. Modern, spacious, with air conditioning – and a maid! Her name was Melita and she became almost part of the family before long. She was particularly fond of Jonathan, who by now was a cute two-year-old. She would go about her cleaning, all the while talking to Jonathan in Maltese. We could never understand anything she said and I'm sure she never understood anything we said either, but somehow we managed to communicate. Mum always told her to help herself to anything in the fridge for lunch, which she did with overwhelming gratitude. The Maltese people were so poor in those days. I used to see them sitting on the beach, rubbing tomato on dry bread, and wondered why they were doing that. "It's because they can't afford to buy much food, so they use one tomato to rub on the bread for all the family" Mum would say. They would shower at the beach because they didn't have bathroom facilities at home.

Malta had been taken over by the British some years earlier, and there was a divided opinion amongst the Maltese as to whether this was a good thing or not. Most of them were glad of the opportunities to be given work by the Brits and to be protected from threatening countries. Others felt they wanted their island back and I remember one day in particular, when we were told to stay indoors because a large group of protesters were roaming the streets throwing stones at the windows of the houses and flats occupied by the British. I remember being horrified by the fact that they shot at birds in the trees, killed them and ate them. I would witness this almost every time we went to the beach or through wooded areas. The best thing was picking fruits and figs to eat from the trees around us. The worst thing was going to the market and seeing chickens and other live animals in cages waiting to be sold for the cooking pot.

So, it was with mixed feelings that we realised this would be our home for the next couple of years. Dad had bought a little car for Mum to use – a Morris Minor. She was delighted but, of course, she did not have a driving licence. Not that it mattered in Malta – there were no rules like that! She managed to drive it from A to B and we were delighted to have an alternative mode of transport to get us round the island.

Mum's Morris Minor

We had been enrolled at the Naval School called Verdala, a distance of about forty minutes by school coach. The school consisted of small huts around a huge playground.

I made new friends quickly and in the summer months school finished at lunchtime. We would return home for a 'siesta' under our mosquito nets until about 4pm after which Mum would take us down the beach. This is where I learned to swim. It was wonderful to have all these beaches at our disposal, and the one we visited more frequently than others was the private beach for Naval Officers. Mainly rocks, but the

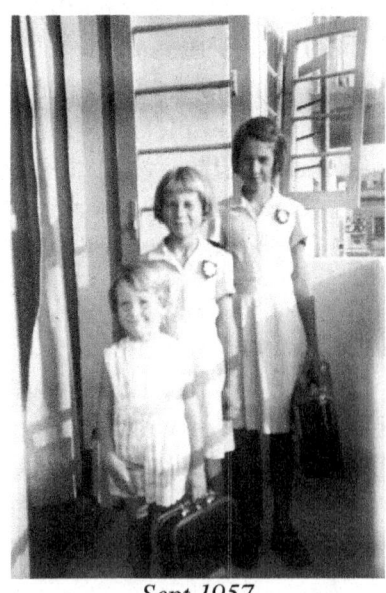

Sept 1957

designated swimming area with a diving board about 60 feet up was my favourite. I would fly off the diving board and disappear deep down into the ocean before coming up for breath.

Yet there was one day when I nearly drowned and I'll never forget the horror of this day for the rest of my life. I had a friend called Susan Garrett. She lived in an apartment down by the quay in the Naval Reserve. One Sunday afternoon we were walking along by the quay near her house. It was a stormy day, wet and windy, and we were watching all the boats bobbing up and down in the harbour. The red flag was flying which was the sign for 'No Swimming'. Anyway, suddenly we noticed that one of the little boats had been ripped away from its mooring and was floating out to sea. We both had this stupid idea to jump in (fully clothed) and bring the boat back. As we swam towards it, the boat went further and further out. We kept swimming until we were able to grab the rope and then started pulling it back to the quayside. The waves were high and vicious and, as we neared the concrete quay, I could see that we were going to be bashed against the concrete. I was terrified. We tried to grab the chains hanging down from the wall but every time I grabbed one, I was ripped out and dragged down by the waves. This happened repeatedly until I couldn't breathe, I lost strength, and I thought to myself, I'm going to drown. Another minute and I would have gone forever. Suddenly, an arm reached down and grabbed me, dragging me out onto the concrete. I looked up, spluttering, to see a man with a dog on the lead. I couldn't speak I was so traumatised. When I got my breath back, I tried to say, 'thank you so much!' but he'd gone. Vanished. Luckily, he pulled Susan out, too. It was a near escape and I never saw the man again to thank him for saving my life. I sometimes wonder if it was my guardian angel that had saved me.

During our time in Malta I was admitted into hospital for an operation. I'd been having sore throats for a long time and it was beginning to affect my attendance at school. In the end the Doctor advised the removal of my tonsils and adenoids. I was told I would get lots of jelly and ice cream, so I didn't put up too much resistance. I remember being in the ward with several other children of my age and it was a straightforward affair - with the promised jelly and ice cream! It was much more common for children to have this operation in those days so it all passed by with hardly a word said.

It was whilst living in Malta that I started to become an avid reader of Enid Blyton. Despite the attempt to get me reading other children's classics, I couldn't give up my infatuation with the adventures of The Famous Five and The Secret Seven. Getting hold of English books was quite difficult in Malta, so I would spend hours scouring the school library, or visiting bookshops to secure the latest Blyton book.

At weekends we would go roller skating along the sea front in Sliema and spend time at the play area. I always took Karen with me – she looked on me as a 'second Mum' and I was very fond of her.

I also became interested in photography. Dad had always been the photographer in our family, he carried the camera almost everywhere. On my 10th birthday I was very excited to be presented with my very first camera - a Brownie camera that went everywhere with me. Dad gave up carrying his camera because he knew I would always be there with mine. I was also developing an interest in pop music. I would save my pocket money to buy the latest disc - I remember the first one I bought - Paul Anka, singing, Diana.

Mum and Dad used to attend cocktail parties and social events on board Ship and also at other people's homes. They also hosted their own cocktail parties quite a lot and, being the eldest, I was always allowed to stay up late and help hand round the cocktails, even join in a game of Totopoly with them. I looked forward to these evenings. I felt very grown up.

I was always being told I looked mature for my age and at the tender age of ten I had a 'boyfriend'. His name was Joey. He was sixteen, and Maltese. I met him at the swings along Sliema seafront. He lived in the house opposite the swings and we used to meet up nearly every day. It was all very naïve and innocent, but I do have a photo of us together to prove I wasn't making it up!

Me and friend Linda   Joey

My parents used to entertain the captain and his wife and also had to mix with other officers, far beyond their social station. I was told later in life that when Dad went for his initial interview with the Admiralty for the promotion to lieutenant commander, Mum was asked to accompany him. She felt that she was being interviewed as well and realised that, unless she could show social graces and talk intelligently, then Dad would not be suitable for this position. They certainly lived up to their station in life.

We had a very privileged life in Malta for those two years. As Dad was a naval officer we were able to use the best facilities at the naval base, such as the swimming pools. Occasionally a day trip to one of the remote beaches was organised on Dad's ship for all the staff and crew. These trips were always great fun. The ship would simply stop somewhere out at sea and we would jump or slide off the side of the ship into the sea and have a lovely swim. Jellyfish were a problem, so we had to keep a look out for them. As Dad was the captain we were allowed privileges – such as going down to the kitchens and asking for cakes.

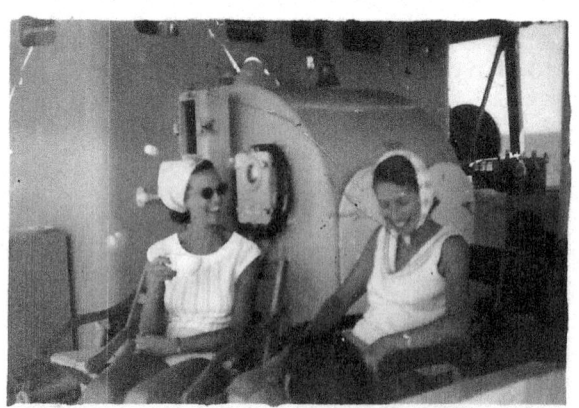

Mum (left) enjoying a joke with the Captain's wife on HMS Fenton

The staff and crew on the ship were always slightly in awe of us kids, just in case one of us complained about any of them!

When Dad was away on patrol we often had a visit from another officer whom we called Uncle Tiger. His name was Oliver Wright and, it would seem, had taken a fancy to Mum. A lot of flirtations and adultery went on in these circles and, unbeknown to me at the time, Mum and Uncle Tiger were having a bit of a harmless fling. He used to arrive with presents for all us children and stay for tea. This continued when we finally arrived back in England, and, I discovered much later, Mum had been tempted to go away with him. I was shocked to discover this, as I knew Mum and Dad loved each other dearly. I think what was lacking in Mum's life was a bit of fun and Dad wasn't up to much of that.

One day we persuaded Mum to let us have a budgerigar. I don't know how it happened, but we ended up with two. One was male, the other female. We thought it would be fun to put a nesting box on the side and see what happened. Sometime later we were totally shocked to find egg in there! We had to keep restraining little Karen and Jonathan from opening the nesting box because we knew that the birds would abandon the egg if they were disturbed too much. Eventually, much to our surprise and joy a little baby bird emerged from this egg! As it was Christmas time we decided to call her 'Cracker'. Cracker was the most precious little thing in our lives. We would cosset her, talk to her, and allow her to fly around the living room. She was so tame she would land on our fingers and sit looking at us with affection. When the time came to pack our bags to return to England, it was unthinkable that we should leave Cracker behind. So she was duly placed in a suitable container and came back home to England with us.

Our time in Malta was drawing to a close. The Government of the UK reached the conclusion that the country was spending more on defence than it could afford or indeed was necessary. Cuts were going to be made and Dad, along with many others, decided to take advantage.

On the beach

The offer being made was a substantial gratuity and a large pension. As he was nearing 40, it was not an option to have any further promotions, so he took the offer. Mum, with four growing children, certainly would appreciate Dad being home more regularly and so, it was with a certain amount of sadness, that Dad withdrew from the service. As he put it: the end of a very pleasant commission and in fact a very pleasant twenty-five years.

We knew that Melita would be heartbroken to see us leave and we decided we would ask her if she would like to return to England with us.

"Oh, no! no! I can't" she wailed. "I have my mother, my sick mother to look after!" She couldn't stop crying and it was with a heavy heart that we bade our farewells and Dad had to mentally prepare himself for civilian life back home.

BACK TO ENGLAND

We were all excited at the prospect of coming home to Emsworth. I remember the first thing I did was to rush to the kitchen sink to turn the tap on for a drink of water. No more boiling! The end of boiling water might have seemed like heaven, however, my return to school was not. I was the 'new girl' once again and I felt socially isolated. All my classmates seemed to have a 'best friend' and it was hard to break into these close friendships. One thing I can remember is the excitement of a teacher arriving one morning with an electrical contraption and announcing, "If you haven't yet seen the new electric kettle, I'm going to show it you now," and she proceeded to plug it in and boil the water. I was astounded! This really was state of the art.

I was almost eleven and the Eleven Plus examination was looming. Mum and Dad obviously hoped, and presumed, I would pass the Eleven Plus and go to Grammar School. All of my class mates had been geared up for the Eleven Plus and, although it was later discovered I was intelligent enough to go to Grammar School, I had not been prepared for this exam.

"I'm afraid you didn't pass," Mum said quietly when the letter had popped through the door. "Never mind, you're not going to

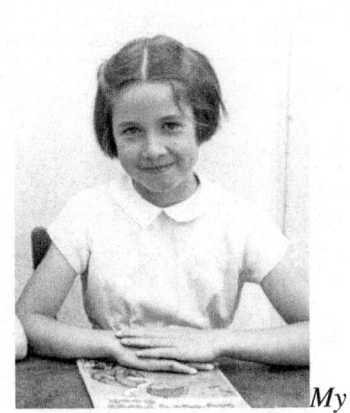

My School photo. I had just had a hair-cut!

57

the Secondary Modern, we'll find a suitable private school for you".

It was during this time that we heard that papa was seriously ill with a brain tumour. Mum had been very close to him and was terribly distressed at the news. All we could do was to wait to hear of any updates. It wasn't long before we heard he had died. He was 69. I will never forget as long as I live the howling I heard from my mother. She could not imagine life without him. He had been very special to all of us. Always full of fun and laughter, despite the cruelty he'd suffered in his lifetime. As the son of an alcoholic mother, he'd been sent away to relatives on numerous occasions where he was often cruelly treated. Then he met my nana, fell in love, and got engaged, but before the wedding could take place he'd been sent off with the Army to the First World War. He kept a photo of her in his breast pocket during the five years he was away and he always believed that is what kept him alive.

Papa on the left before departure for war.

The Liverpool King's Regiment were sent to France and endured the most horrific conditions. Survival was a miracle. Yet papa had a very kind, compassionate, and sensitive nature, and he insisted on staying on the battlefield to rescue any soldier that appeared to be alive. For this he was awarded the Military

Medal.

After the war he married his beloved fiancé and spoiled her and his three daughters throughout his life. He could not abide cruelty or neglect. I've been told, he would visit the houses of the rich to ask for any unwanted clothing. Then he would go to the Docks area and distribute the clothing to the most needy. At Christmas he would always invite anybody who was on their own to come and spend it at Anstey Road. It must have been very difficult for him as a police officer, to deal with the crimes and neglect in Liverpool in those days. Mum travelled to his funeral on her own. She was devastated and decided it was not appropriate for us children to attend the funeral at our age.

Meanwhile, Dad had to prepare himself for applying for a job, which was difficult considering he had no training or experience in anything other than the navy. He had received his gratuity of £6,000 (equivalent of £300,000 now) and we were free to move wherever we liked. After applying for various vacancies, he finally decided on a job opportunity with John Lewis as an assistant manager of the electrical appliance department at their store in Southampton, Tyrell & Green.

Greenways was put on the market and a new house sought in the Southampton area. I felt sad to leave Greenways, it had been a fun place to live but our next adventure was just about to start, and I wondered which school awaited me. A pleasant house in Chandlers Ford was to be our destination, for the time being anyway. A large, four bedroomed detached house with a lovely garden at the back. £4,000, the price, apparently.

As it was, No.13. The name "Touchwood" was added to the front porch.

I had been enrolled at The Gregg School in Southampton, a journey of about ten miles. Dad took me to school each morning and I caught the bus back in the afternoon. It was a mixed school and I settled in quite quickly. The discipline seemed harsh. I can still remember us all standing to attention in silence if the headmaster walked through the playground during our break. If any of the rules were broken (which included not wearing your school hat on the way home), the consequences were dire. Boys would be thrashed with a cane. The amount of homework given every night was huge. Two hours every evening and three at the weekend. Dad was very patient with me

New uniform

and spent many hours poring over my Maths and English homework. I was still not a fan of playing sports and would get out of hockey or tennis whenever I could.

I was thirteen when I managed to persuade Mum and Dad to let me have a dog. Julia had her cat, Karen pampered her guinea pig, rabbits, and mice. I wanted a dog. After much searching and waiting, we eventually found the perfect puppy. A family just up the road, living in a huge house, had three puppies for sale. The mother was an Old English Sheepdog and the father a black Labrador. The puppies, although from two pedigree parents, were being sold for just a few pounds each. I eagerly ran up the drive to view them. All three pups came running out and I knew immediately which one was 'mine'. He was the only one with a shaggy coat like his mother! He was so adorable. I scooped him up in my arms and announced, "This one is mine!". We called him Fluffy. Fluffy became a much-loved part of our family and travelled everywhere with us. He had

Fluffy with the children

a gentle nature and gave us so much pleasure.

Opposite our house lived a family of five small children. The youngest, was about 12 months old, and the eldest, a nine-year-old. We often played with them and I remember several times pushing the baby out in the pram, down to the woods where we would all slide down the embankment on a flat piece of wood. We did this often. I'm amazed that any mother would allow a twelve-year-old to take her little baby out down to the woods with a crowd of other children. I think she was glad to see the back of them all, so she could have some peace. The following year they moved away. To Eastbourne I think.

One day when I came home from school I notice our budgie, Cracker, was not in his cage.

"Where's Cracker, Mum?" I asked.

"Oh, she was off her food, so I thought it best to take her to the vets. She should be back tomorrow, all being well". I thought no more about it, she was only two years old and I presumed she would be back in her cage the following day. But, to our dismay, we got a phone call the following day.

"I'm sorry" the vet said compassionately, "but there was nothing we could do. Cracker had an egg stuck in the wrong place and we had to put her down". We couldn't believe it. I cried for days. It was like losing a family member.

We had frequent visitors. My nana would come and stay for a couple of weeks every six months, and even my great-grandmother, Sarah, came down with her once on the coach. She would have been in her early 80's. By then, Auntie Mavis had managed to start leading a fairly normal life after her trauma down in the air raid shelter, although she was forgetful and irrational at times. However, she had met and fallen in love with a very handsome young man called Les. By the time we were living in Chandlers Ford they had two little boys and they occasionally came to visit us. Sadly, the marriage didn't last. A couple of years later Les walked out on her, leaving her with the two boys and no money. My nana had to move in with her and help her to cope. Les had suffered much in his marriage, which was probably understandable, but our family never spoke to him again.

Great Grandma Sarah and my nana May would visit us regularly

On Sundays we always went to Sunday School. I can't remember whether I enjoyed going or not but by the age of twelve I was allowed to decide on my out-of-school activities and pastimes. I remember being confirmed at the local church there. It was more like a church hall. Soon afterwards, the vicar approached me.

"How would you like to be one of the junior Sunday School teachers, Christine?" I was totally shocked. Me? Apparently, there was a shortage of teachers.

"Well, yes, thank you very much," I stuttered. I used to walk down to the reverend's house one evening a week to learn and reflect my 'lesson' for the following Sunday. It made me feel quite important and, being used to looking after my three younger brother and sisters, this was really just an extension of that!

On Sunday afternoons, Mum and Dad used to like us to go for a family walk. I hated these boring walks with a passion. It was never very interesting, just walking around the local area usually. Most families seemed to do this on Sunday afternoons.

"Mum," I said one dismal dull Sunday morning, "I don't want to come on a walk this afternoon. How about I stay here and I'll have the tea all ready for you all when you get back". Mum was quite happy with this arrangement, so every Sunday for the next year or so, I would stand in the kitchen making lots of sandwiches, chocolate cake and jelly (always the same), and lay the table so it was all ready for them at about 5pm when they returned. It gave me so much pleasure to see them all tuck in. And Mum was forever grateful for this break from the kitchen! She told people about it for years afterwards.

I had a go at horse riding and after several lessons decided it wasn't really something I wanted to pursue. I did a paper round for a very short time, Mum and Dad were very consistent in their view that all money should be earned. To get our pocket money we had to clean our bedrooms and do other chores like going to the shops or helping in the kitchen. I loved going ice-skating on the rink in Southampton which I did regularly with my friends.

Our summer holidays were simple. One year we rented a caravan in the West Country, so we could take Fluffy with us. Another year Mum decided it might be good to go to Butlin's Holiday Camp where she could let us loose and she would have a bit of peace! I was 12, Julia 10, Karen 6 and Jonathan 4. She chose a camp in Pwllheli, North Wales. We were thrilled and couldn't wait to get there. We were housed in a little chalet and had the whole place at our disposal. Funfair, swimming pools, entertainment, etc. etc. Unfortunately, Mum hated every minute of it.

"Can't stand this constant noise and crowds," she complained. "Never again!" Mealtimes in the dining room were the occasions she hated the most. A real "Hi De Hi!"

"Right" muttered Dad "I'll choose the holiday next time then!"

On holiday in Wales

By the time I was thirteen, going on fourteen, I was getting increasingly interested in pop music, particularly Cliff and the Shadows. I saved all my pocket money to buy their records and magazines. One day I decided to enter a competition which was advertised on the back of a Crosse & Blackwell tin of something. It was for youngsters up to age 14 and the question was "If you were living on a desert island, and you were only allowed to take one thing, what would it be?" The first prize was a record player! Second prize a bicycle. I wanted both. I didn't hesitate to enter the competition. After thinking long and hard about what my answer should be, I suddenly had a 'brain wave'. We'd been learning in science at school about a device that could turn sea water into fresh water and I chose that. I couldn't believe it when the results popped through the front door.

"Wow! Look at this! I've won First Prize!" When a record player duly arrived in the post a few days later, I was thrilled and took it with me wherever we moved from that day to when I finally sold it in 2006.

Mum and Dad were often out at the same time, so I would be expected to entertain the three children. I would make dens for them, do gardening with them, take Fluffy for walks, make cakes and biscuits. I learned to be creative. By

Fluffy was one amazing dog.

this time we had a dog, a cat, and seventeen guinea pigs! We had started out with three, one each for me, Julia, and Karen. Unbeknown to us, one of them was a female, so the first litter arrived quite quickly. Then another litter and another, before we finally managed to find a home for most of them. We had a large dolls house in the garden with a big wire run and we'd leave them out there.

If one escaped, as often happened, Fluffy would run after it and pick it up by the scruff of its neck and bring it back.

At weekends I decided it might be a good idea to start running occasional jumble sales for the neighbours to come and buy stuff we didn't want. We had so much in the way of old clothes, toys, books that were no longer needed, so I had this idea to write little newsletters and post them through the doors of the neighbours to encourage them to come along. Looking back, I was quite the entrepreneur, but I also saw it as a way of amusing the younger children.

"Go and find all the toys and books you don't want" I would call, "and put them in a box in the garage." I wrote newsletters to distribute around the neighbours which included the date of the sale, then we would get fold up tables, place them around the lawn in the garden and pile them with stuff. I would even make toffee and biscuits to sell. Such excitement on the day! A few neighbours, mainly other children, would pour into the garden to browse around and buy some of the bits and pieces. I loved it. We all did. Fluffy would run madly around greeting everyone. Afterwards we would count up how much money we had made and shared it between us.

Meanwhile, Dad was becoming somewhat disenchanted with his job. Boring and predictable – just what Dad didn't like. During his time in the store he had been introduced to a new and innovative product called Colston, a small dishwasher that would sit on the draining board and wash dishes for four people. It had been produced by the man who had been the chairman, and managing director of Hoover, Sir Charles Colston. The price was just £89. Dad thought there was a huge potential for this product and that possibly every home would have one in the future. An opportunity came for him to join the company, so long as he agreed to be one of the Sales Representatives. He applied for the position and waited several months before he learned he was successful and that he could start the following June. Two weeks training in Surrey and a red and yellow Morris Minor van with 'Colston' written across it came with the job. Apparently, Dad felt very embarrassed driving this van around and hoped he didn't run into anyone he knew! He was responsible for the Southampton/New Forest/Winchester area, and his job was to call on dealers who stocked the machine to keep their interest and enthusiasm high. Demonstrations had to be organised, both in public places and also in people's homes. He enjoyed the job and did so well that the following year when a National Contest was held he was presented with a huge silver cup for being the Sales Representative who sold the most dishwashers.

In the spring of 1962 Dad received a telephone call from the Service Manager of the West Country who asked to speak to him. The reason for the visit was to ask Dad if he would be willing to be area manager of the West Country as the results of the sales in that area were not satisfactory. Of course this would mean our whole family moving once again. Mum always wanted to support Dad in any decision he made, particularly when it came to his career, so plans began for a move down to the Exeter area. I was devastated to say the least. I had made good friends at my school, I loved the area where we lived. Thirteen is a difficult age to make a transition and I told them I wasn't going! I said I would live with our neighbour across the road. I seriously meant it. I couldn't bear the thought of leaving my school and my friends and all that I had built up in Chandlers Ford. I hated my parents for this decision. Yet in the end I realised, realistically, I had no choice. I was told I would be enrolled at a convent in Exmouth. I sunk more and more into my love of pop music, joining fan clubs and going to concerts whenever I could. I started writing to pen pals around the country and asking if I could come and stay. I was beginning to feel like a Nomad. No particular place to go.

All kitted out in our new uniforms. Me, Julia, and Karen to the Convent. Jonathan obviously not keen on his new gear!

The winter of 1962/3 was one of the worst on record. Thick snow engulfed the whole country. We were moving in the middle of it. Dad put chains round the wheels of the car and we all wondered if we would make the 200-mile journey to Exeter. On the day we moved, my six-year-old brother,

Jonathan, stood outside on the road and said, "I can't see any flags Mummy". We all laughed as Mum remembered saying a few days earlier, "The neighbours will put the flags out on the day we leave."

So, with four children and a dog, off we went to the West Country. It was a slow and laborious journey with frequent stops to wipe the snow off the car and let the dog out for some fresh air. I had Karen on my lap, Julia had Jonathan on hers. No seat belts in those days! After what seemed like an eternity we finally arrived at our new home in Exmouth.

I hardly had time to put up my Cliff and The Shadows posters on the wall before I was being driven off to my new school, the Exmouth Convent. What an extraordinary contrast to my previous school in Southampton! Nuns floating around giving orders. Girls, wearing childish short white socks and sandals, on their best behaviour. Worst of all the academic level at this school was way beyond my comprehension. I was completely out of my depth. Not knowing anybody only added to my distress. I sunk into despair and wondered how I would cope or carry on.

I have no memory of my time in Exmouth, only the relief when, three months later, Dad announced we would be moving over to Berkshire. He had been offered a further promotion, manager for the Home Counties, and of course he could not possibly turn it down. My relief was short lived. I knew my parents had been to see the Mother Superior about my level of attainment and potential, but I was not prepared to hear them come home and tell me their decision.

Mum turned to me and said "The Mother Superior says you are an intelligent and conscientious girl. She thinks that once you've caught up with the others, you'd benefit from staying as a boarder rather than changing schools once again."

I was horrified! Surely they didn't mean to leave me behind at this awful place, as a BOARDER! I summoned all the defiance within me and shouted, "I'd never consider staying there! If you make me stay I'll run away!" I stormed off to my bedroom to sulk. A few days of tension ensued as I reiterated my intention to run away should they make me stay. Finally they could see my distress and I was told I could go with them to Berkshire after all.

Winnersh, near Wokingham, was our next home. A pleasant newly built detached house was found, and my parents were to contact the local authorities to see if they could get me into the Grammar School there. I was told I would need to take an exam. I took it and passed. Mum and Dad were delighted, so off I went with enthusiastic optimism to my last and final school. I was almost fifteen and had no idea what lay in front of me.

Fifteen is a difficult age; hormones are surging. The transition from child to adult is complicated enough without the extra stress of moving to a completely new area. Being thrown into a new school where most pupils had known each other for at least four years, was very disconcerting. The fact I'm very sensitive did not help either, and my stress began to manifest itself as stomach pains and withdrawal. My parents became very worried about my state of health and took me to numerous doctors, even a psychiatrist. I sank deeper and deeper into the love of my life – my obsession with pop stars such as: Adam Faith, Cliff & The Shadows, The Beatles, Billy Fury, etc.etc. I would get myself to their shows and concerts, even if it meant a train journey to Central London. One night I decided I wanted to see Jimi Hendrix on stage. I travelled by myself, intending to get the last train home at around 11pm. The show was fantastic, I heard and saw sights I'd never seen before: people rocking on drugs, making love in the corners of the room, black and white flashing lights, and very loud music. I loved every minute of it. I was so engrossed in the atmosphere I missed the last train home! I stayed and enjoyed it until it finished, probably around 3pm. Then I trundled off to the station to catch the first train to Reading. I knew my parents would be worried stiff and I hoped they hadn't called out the police. Luckily for me, they hadn't, but when I walked in the door at 6am they were absolutely furious to say the least.

"All this worry you've given us, you irresponsible girl, have you any idea what danger you could have put yourself in?"

I woke up the next day deciding I needed to be more independent and earn some money of my own. As I was becoming more interested in pop records, I applied for a Saturday job at the local record shop and I got it. 15/- for the day. I could listen to pop songs all day and buy records at the end of it.

The biggest shock of all came when I arrived for my first day at my new school, the Holt Grammar School, in Wokingham. Arriving in my socks and sandals, I felt stupid, humiliated in fact, to see my fellow pupils all wearing stockings and heels. These girls looked about eighteen and I looked about twelve. Nobody spoke to me and the head teacher was really strict and unmerciful. I quickly realised too that I was ahead in some subjects but behind in others. It seemed like a nightmare, but I had to keep reminding myself that I only had eighteen months at this awful institution and I could leave when I was sixteen. I kept my head down and tried to ignore the disdainful stares of the other girls. Mum engaged the services of a private tutor, so I could catch up with the subjects in which I was struggling I immersed myself in books from the library and my all-time favourite was The Interpretation of Dreams by Freud. How amazing, I thought, that someone can interpret dreams.

I became increasingly interested in how the mind worked. Psychology, yes, that was it. I decided I wanted to be a psychologist when I left school. I read numerous books on the subject, none of which interested any other members of my family. I found it fascinating that one person in a family can 'inherit' a love of something, and yet others not show any interest in the subject at all. This led me to believe that we inherit our gifts, talents, and the choices we make, through the genes we get from our parents, grandparents or even great-grandparents. I've spent many hours researching this subject during my lifetime and the conclusions reached by research keep changing by the decade. I always used to wonder why a someone may give birth to a talented, gifted, obedient child, and then their second child turns out to be a criminal or even a murderer. Some people believe it is how a child is treated, and others believe it is all in the genes. I tend to believe the genes play 75% role in our character and personality, the other 25% is conditioning. It's a subject I've enjoyed debating many times over the years. A study was developed a few years ago using identical twins who had never known each other, they were separated at the beginning of the war and sent to different adoptive parents. The conclusion that was reached was that we inherit 50% from our upbringing and 50% our genes.

My feelings of isolation in school changed soon after I had met the one and only George Harrison. I was suddenly very popular, and many girls wanted to know more about this meeting. One girl in particular, called Barbara, became my best friend. She was a 'secret' mad Beatles fan and suddenly we were spending time with each other, reminiscing about old concerts and television programmes that we'd watched. We started making plans to go to Beatles concerts whenever we could. I began to feel happier than I had done in a long, long time.

The 2i's Coffee Bar in Soho was popular at the time. Many famous names had started their career there. One day I asked Barbara if she'd like to come with me. I didn't tell Mum and Dad where I was going, I knew they wouldn't approve. We had a great day, admired all the signed discs on the walls and couldn't wait to tell our friends at school all about it. My favourite TV programme at the time was Ready Steady Go. Lulu was a frequent singer, along with many other famous names. The audience would dance around, and I thought how wonderful it would be to go there. I applied for two tickets and – to my amazement – got them! I went with Julia. It was certainly a memorable occasion. I can't remember who was on the stage at the time, but it was all going out live on TV.

My GCE exams were looming and I endeavoured to do my best, as Mum had always reminded me. My work improved, I particularly enjoyed English Language, English Literature, Biology, and French. I struggled with Maths and hated Science. I must have done something right, however, because the following term it was announced that I would be head girl for the class year. I couldn't believe it, but I didn't want to lose friends over this. My worst fear was that they might think I was a 'goody-goody'. The school organised a trip to Switzerland the following spring and I was delighted to learn that I could go. I think this helped deepen some of my friendships with the other girls, thus my fears about becoming head-girl were pacified.

One of the highlights of that summer was a trip to Yorkshire to visit a newly made penfriend, Anne. She lived near Haworth, the home of the Bronte sisters. As I had been avidly reading their books, I was thrilled to have the opportunity to visit the parsonage where they lived. I still remember walking around there – a village almost untouched since the day they left. I recall walking into the rooms where they wrote their famous stories, gazing through the same windows that they had looked out of, and being fascinated as I gently touched the walls and furniture. It seemed surreal. A very special visit.

Meanwhile, Dad was proving to be a very successful sales manager for Colston. Sales were on average somewhere between 250 to 300 per week and, in the period running up to Christmas, as many as 750, for which Dad became the toast of the company. He was invited to Michael Colston's manor house near Nettlebed, Oxfordshire, for dinner with all the trimmings. These dinners became a regular event, with Mum being invited as well.

As Dad writes: These dinners resulted in many an amusing evening as Michael Colston was a man of extreme snobbishness who seemed to go out of his way to make those of lesser good fortune feel uncomfortable.

No matter how stressful a year had been we always had our fun Christmas to look forward to in Liverpool. We would pack our warmest clothes, take all our carefully wrapped presents and the six of us would pile into the car for the long journey. When reaching the Mersey Tunnel, we would all whoop with delight. A warm welcome greeted us, the old kettle would be put on for tea and we would talk and eat, talk and eat until late into the night. When my grandfather was alive he was such a comedian; he would carry out practical tricks on us children and play games until we were exhausted. He never knew that one day, his great nephew would turn out to be Britain's most highly paid comedian. More on that later.

Aunts, uncles, and cousins would arrive, or we would visit them. There was more laughter, presents, and cuddles and the proverbial exclamation of, "Haven't you grown!" Occasionally we would have Christmas dinner with my great-grandparents. They had a small end of terraced house in Rathbone Road, where we would run in through the backyard into their kitchen/dining room and all sit round chatting and reminiscing. The 'front parlour' was kept for special occasions and as Christmas was a special occasion, we were allowed to sit in it. In fact, all of us children, including the cousins, would sit patiently whilst the 'grown ups' had their dinner first. Then we would be allowed to come back into the other room to eat. We were always good mannered and never spoke out of turn. That is how we were brought up - somewhat unlike most of today's children, I feel. At my grandparents I would share a bed with Julia. Karen and Jonathan squeezed in with Mum and Dad in another bedroom. It was tight but somehow we managed it. We were always sad when we had to leave.

When the day of my GCE's arrived, I didn't feel very confident. I was hoping to get at least four. To get five or more in those days would ensure a place at University. In the event, I passed three, English Language, Biology and French. So, my intention of becoming a psychologist would have to wait. I enrolled at the local college for a one-year course in commercial typing and bookkeeping. Before then, we took a holiday to Spain, driving across France and staying overnight in hotels. So my knowledge of the French language certainly helped. I was the only one in the family who could work out where to go or what to eat!

I remember a trip to Ireland with Barbara that summer. I was never sure why it was I chose Northern Ireland, but I believe I wanted to visit the mountains of Mourne. It may have been a book I'd been reading that inspired me to go, or just the fact that they were supposed to be extremely spectacular. So, one sunny summer afternoon Barbara and I caught the ferry across to Belfast. The plan was to hitch hike down to Armagh, staying overnight in youth hostels on the way. I was only sixteen, I imagine Mum and Dad were not comfortable with the whole thing, yet I had my own mind and was determined to do it. The scenery was just as stunning as I had expected; rolling hills; green, green grass; beautiful sunsets, and magical atmosphere. One incident occurred that almost ruined the whole adventure. We had been given a lift by a group of teenagers and we must have been having such a good time that we went off with them in the evening and totally forgot to check the time. Doors always closed at the youth hostels at 10pm. We returned at 10.30pm. There was nobody around; it was all in complete darkness.

"What shall we do?" I wailed to Barbara, watching the car load of teenagers disappear into the horizon.

"No option but to make ourselves comfortable on the floor of the porch and sleep here," replied Barbara wearily. So that's what we did. We had an uncomfortable, cold night until we were let in the following morning at 7am when we could grab some breakfast and an hour's sleep before being turfed out again.

Meanwhile at home Mum was becoming increasingly irritated by the noise coming from the secondary school behind our house. Our garden literally overlooked their playing fields and for much of the day she was forced to endure the shouts and screams of the teenagers, constantly playing sports and games. Eventually she decided we needed to move to a quieter location, so the house was put on the market and she started scouting the area for something suitable. A three-bedroomed detached bungalow was found at Sonning on Thames, a pretty village in a particularly sought-after area due to its proximity to the Thames and to Reading. It had a large garden and a field at the back where Karen could keep her pony which she had acquired the previous year.

New house in Sonning

We moved in the following spring. The bungalow was unheated, with just one coal fire in the living room. I remember waking up to find ice forming on the inside of my bedroom window. I'd been enjoying my course at college; my shorthand and typing speeds were excellent and I was assured I could easily get a job in September. My social life had taken a turn for the worse as far as Mum and Dad were concerned. I'd made a new friend, a party girl called Carol, who went to parties every weekend and had numerous boyfriends. I'd never had a boyfriend, and at sixteen, going on seventeen, I decided it was about time I did. I started going to parties with her and it wasn't long before I was dating boys on a regular basis, much to my parent's dismay as I didn't tell them where I was going or how long I would be. I would walk down to the river and meet a boy who lived at the lock. Carol had already dated him for a short time. John and I became close very quickly. We'd go on the bus to town to the cinema, go to a dance, walk along the river, listen to music together, lie on the river bank in the sunshine. We fell head over heels in love and I wanted to spend all my spare time with him. He had been a pupil at the expensive private school in Sonning and

Christine & John 1965

was now looking for a job. Trouble was that he didn't really want to find one. He wanted to be free to wander. He'd borrow a scooter from a friend and go off somewhere, only returning to eat and see me. I tried to introduce him to Mum and Dad, but it was obvious they didn't approve of him.

"What? No job? No money? Sounds like a layabout to me." Dad would stamp around in disgust. I took no notice and continued to date him.

That summer as I was visiting my friend Patricia in Wokingham, I suddenly had a thought, "Do you fancy going to Italy?" I asked her. "It's cheaper than most other places and we could laze on the beaches in the sun and go to nightclubs in the evening."

Patricia jumped at the chance and we immediately set about arranging our trip. It was something John couldn't consider as he never had any money. Mum was worried. "Don't speak to any boys on the beach, will you? They might follow you back to your Hotel and cause a problem! Always stay together. Don't wander off on your own." Lots of good advice, which – in those days – was probably wise. The tourist industry had not really started and it was fairly uncommon to see English people in Europe, particularly two young attractive girls on their own. Most Italians couldn't speak a word of English. Off we went, it was a wonderful week. I remembered Mum's advice and avoided wandering off with any of the attentive boys – of which there were many.

In the September I found a job as Junior Secretary with Adwest Engineering, near Reading. I started with much enthusiasm and hoped my ability to carry out the job met with approval. I was 'under the wing' of the senior secretary, who seemed to treat me with contempt from day one. She was not at all friendly, and never acknowledged anything I did for her. I felt frustrated and disappointed. Is this what working life was like? I put up with it for three months and then decided to look elsewhere. A vacancy was going with Thomas Cook Travel Agents. I jumped at it. What a contrast! Lively staff, who appreciated everything I did, and my confidence started to creep back up.

One night, John and I went to see Manfred Mann in Reading. It was a fantastic concert, everyone was up dancing and I completely lost track of time. Again. We missed the last bus home. I had to call Dad to ask him to come and get us. He was furious! I was told this would be the last time I could go out in the evening with John and that until I learned to be more responsible then I should not see him at all. This had the opposite effect on me and John and I discussed going away together. We'd been dating for over a year and we imagined it would only be a matter of time before we got married. Little did I know what was in store for me. I knew John had insecurity problems which stemmed from the fact he was adopted as a three-year-old. He never felt loved by his adopted mother. He was constantly searching for his real mother, an impossible task in those days where records were kept secret. Consequently, he hung on to me like a bud on a flower and I was giving him all the security he craved.

A short time later I started experiencing severe lower stomach pains. They became so intense I had to stop work and was advised by the doctor to go to hospital. The diagnosis was appendicitis. I had to face an operation to remove my appendix and spend six weeks at home recovering. It was a grim time and I missed John terribly.

Then came the news that was to change my life. Mum and Dad announced, after some consideration, that they had decided we would have a better life in New Zealand. Arrangements would be made as soon as possible to emigrate. I was shocked to the core. Leave John? No! No! No! I told them I would not be coming with them. They ignored me and booked us all a passage on the Angelina Lauro, leaving Southampton in November. This decision had come about for several reasons, mainly because of Dad's job with Colston. As Sales Manger he was dealing with enquiries coming from New Zealand who wanted to know if they could manufacture and sell their own machines. Importing dishwashers from England to New Zealand was not an option under the import restrictions in place at that time. Michael Colston decided to bring in a Marketing Manager for this job and Dad would be directly under him as Senior Sales Representative. Dad was not happy about this at all. He decided to contact the company wanting to sell dishwashers in New Zealand and offer his services in the Marketing, Manufacturing and Service capacity. A job was offered that would ensure his present salary provided he could get the licence that they needed. He lost no time in accepting the position and started the process to emigrate. Added to this, Mum had been visited by a distant relative from the South Island who extolled the virtues and climate of this wonderful country. Jonathan was under pressure at school and was physically going downhill. Dad believed that Julia was out of control, galivanting around with boys in nightclubs, and obviously they wanted me to forget John. The land of sunshine beckoned! British people were being encouraged to emigrate to Australia and New Zealand in those days and you could travel for only £10 on a Government sponsored deal. Unfortunately we did not qualify for that as Dad was earning too much.

A photo to give to my nana in her garden before leaving for New Zealand

I was heartbroken at the thought of leaving John. We both were. I knew I had no option and lay awake at night wondering how I would ever get over it. The house was sold, and the packing began. Of course we would take our beloved Fluffy with us. The hardest thing would be to say

Angelino Lauro

goodbye to my nana and all the other relatives in Liverpool. Mum made a solemn promise that we would pay for nana to come and visit us the following year.

NEW ZEALAND

The journey by ship was six weeks and was an epic adventure in itself. We had paid for good cabins with windows, the food was excellent, the entertainment, the cinema, the library, the games on deck, the swimming pool – it was all far beyond our expectations. As we travelled to all the ports around Europe, picking up families from different countries, we soon realised that they would all be getting off in Australia. Only the British were going to New Zealand. The rules for emigration in those days were strict. To enter New Zealand, you had to be British, middleclass, and with a job already in the pipeline, whereas anybody could go to Australia, no matter what nationality or reason. The days seemed endless as we sailed across the seas. We stopped at Port Said before entering the Suez Canal. We had a short time ashore and when I spotted a pair of bongos I pounced on them. Now I could do some drumming! The journey through the canal was interesting. Dad had camped during the war at Ismailia on the banks, so he was familiar with the area. After travelling through the Red Sea, we sailed around southern Yemen and on to Aden where we had a twenty four hour stop scheduled.

Aden was in a state of chaos. It was in the process of passing from being a British protectorate to part of Saudi Arabia. The British were still in control but the whole place was riddled with armed British Army personnel. Mum refused to go ashore.

"I'm not risking everything to walk down there amongst all those thieves!" she announced. But Dad wanted to go, and, after a short hesitation, I decided to go with him. It felt unsafe to be away from the ship, so after a short time strolling amongst the poor begging natives, we quickly made our way back.

From Aden it was on to Colombo, Sri Lanka and then ten days at sea before we reached Perth in Australia.

We watched whales swimming alongside the ship; gazed at the beautiful sunsets at night, and never forgot to walk Fluffy on the dog deck whenever we could. All the time I thought about John and wrote letters to him almost daily.

Passing through Aden

We stopped at Freemantle and visited Perth, which we all loved, and then on to Melbourne where a very special meeting had been arranged. My great-uncle, Eddie, brother of my beloved grandfather, Ernie, Mum's father, had emigrated to Australia in 1924 and although he had kept in touch by letters to the family, he had never returned to England, nor met any of his relatives since that time. It was an extremely emotional meeting. Ernie had died seven years previous to our meeting with Eddie and Mum could not stop the flow of tears as she hugged Eddie for the first time in her life. He had landed in Melbourne, aged 24, with just a shilling in his pocket – so we had been told. He managed to get a job as a sheep farmer on land about 200 miles from Melbourne and this is where he had lived and worked all his life. He was in his mid sixties and looked worn out and bedraggled. Never married, he had never seen any news nor read any newspapers since the day he had left England.

I took a photo with him on my polaroid camera and gave it to him. We spent the day with him and it was a sad goodbye when we left. He kept in touch by letter until he died in the early 70's, leaving Mum and several other relatives a share of the money raised from the sale of his land. It was a substantial amount and Mum was astounded to receive it. Little did we know that the story of Eddie and his life would be shown on BBC TV in 2013 – which I will come back to later.

This was a monumental occasion for both him and us

Next stop was Sydney where a shock was in store for Dad. A letter was waiting for him from the company in New Zealand that had offered him a job. It blandly stated that they were unable to continue with the Colston product and therefore there was no job for him! It was a hard blow. Unbelievable to think that we would soon be arriving in New Zealand with no job and nowhere to go. I remember Mum and Dad said that they found the people in Sydney to be rude and impolite and were glad to leave. Three days later the dogs all started barking furiously on the dog deck.

"They can smell the land in the distance long before we see it," Dad told us.

At last, Wellington harbour came into sight and we had reached our destination. We could now get off the ship and begin our new life.

AUCKLAND

The plan was to drive up to Auckland and secure a house, but only Dad and I were going there first. Mum and the younger children were to get a coach to her great-aunt Vi in Pukekohe. "We'll stay overnight," Mum told the kids. "Aunt Violet is in her 80's so we need to be polite and very quiet when we arrive."

It was Vi who had inspired Mum to consider New Zealand as a future home when she had visited England a few years earlier. Her father, John, was one of the Evitts, the family of which had emigrated there in the 1860's to help fight the Maori wars. Originally from Ireland, the sons were all in the army and were expected to help seal New Zealand for the British. John Evitt had discharged himself from the army shortly after arriving in New Zealand and opened a gun shop in the centre of Auckland, selling all kinds of weapons. A replica of his gun shop can still be seen in the Military Museum in Auckland – a place I visited myself in 2008.

According to the rest of the family, the journey to Pukekohe on the coach was one long nightmare. The tiny coach was not built for the narrow, bumpy winding roads that trailed up and down the hills.

Apparently, Julia was worried about the being attacked by natives. "Will the Maoris come down and attack us from the mountains?"

"Yes, and take us to the cooking pot!" joked Mum. Eventually the coach dumped them all off in Pukekohe with all their luggage and they were left stranded trying to locate a taxi to take them to Vi's house. Arriving late in the evening, it was dark and quiet at Aunt Vi's. No sound of anyone or anything could be heard. The place seemed deserted. They knocked. Nothing. They knocked repeatedly. Still nothing. Eventually a man came to door.

"What's going on out here?!" he demanded.

"Where is Vi?" Mum asked, "We've just come off the ship from England and have come to see her".

"Vi is ill in bed. I'm helping her. She's not expecting anyone!" They were eventually taken in and stayed the night, but it was obvious they were not wanted. The next morning, after a brief chat with Vi about family history they left by taxi. Mum, and the rest of us, were never to see Vi again.

Meanwhile Dad and I had driven up to Auckland to find a motel to accommodate us. Mum and the others joined us the following day. "You can't bring the dog in here!" announced the man on reception. "It'll have to sleep in the car". Poor Fluffy. He wondered what on earth was going on.

The first priority was for Dad to find a suitable job. We were limited (by law) to stay no longer than about a month in the motel before moving to a permanent residence so Dad lost no time in applying for jobs. A possibility was with Smith and Brown Ltd. as Section Manager for home appliances and buyer for the company's nineteen stores. He was successful in his application, but before starting the job he had to deal with the managing director who was obviously annoyed and angry that someone from England had sailed in and taken a management post. Despite this hostility, Dad took up his position and found the staff in the store most helpful.

Meanwhile, a search for a suitable home was intensifying. We were introduced to a Mr. Laury Knott – a cheerful and helpful man – who eventually became a lifelong friend of ours. He proudly showed us a large four-bedroom detached house in Howick, about five miles south of Auckland. It was within walking distance of a beautiful bay that overlooked Rangitoto Island.

"We'll take it," Mum told Laury as though her life depended on it. "We can move in straight away".

"Righto," Laury replied. "Let's get started then! Where's your furniture?" It wasn't long before all our furniture and belongings arrived in crates and we soon made ourselves comfortable.

Our house in Howick

It was mid-summer and the children often went to school barefoot. Karen was enrolled at the local girls' high school. Julia and I both got secretarial jobs in Auckland city. Mine was with the Auckland Savings Bank, in the typing pool. A friendly bunch of folk, easy going and fun. There was a lot of laughter and I quickly made friends. My heart was still broken after having to leave John, but I decided I needed to move on and attract a new boyfriend. There was plenty of opportunity for that, but somehow it didn't happen.

It was becoming obvious that Dad's wages would not cover all our needs and would definitely not enable us to send money to my grandmother to visit us. He found his job boring and particularly unpleasant with the managing director's attitude towards him.

Dad in his boat

"Why don't you buy a small boat and go fishing?" Mum suggested one day. "I'll try and get a job to supplement our income".

Jonathan, who was now twelve, had joined the sailing club nearby. Mum found herself a job as a wages controller in a large company. Her wages enabled them to buy Jonathan a sailing boat of his own and he was soon participating in races around the bay. A beautiful Palomino horse was bought for Karen – her love of horses never diminished.

I would enjoy skipping down to the bay whenever possible and swim and sunbathe on the beach. We were picking fruit off the trees and generally life was much less stressful than in England. The land of the 'long White Cloud' – so it is known. Full of sunshine and warmth, a near perfect climate. No class distinction, everyone lived side by side and were 'mates'. It seemed like a blissful existence.

A few months later I was at work, about to head off for lunch when someone came running up the stairs at me. "Christine! There is someone to see you. Outside the front door on the street." I wondered who on earth it could be. As I stepped outside the front door, in the bright sunshine I squinted with shock. It was John! I was speechless.

"I thought I'd surprise you," he said, laughing. How are you, darling?"

I felt I was dreaming as I slid my arm into his and we scurried down the road in search of a place to sit down and talk. "Why didn't you tell me? Where did you get the money for the fare?".

He'd wanted to surprise me, and he did that all right. His explanation of where he got the money – borrowed from his mother – seemed a bit farfetched. My heart was pounding with joy, but my brain was saying, this is not going to work…

I went home to consider what to do. Do I run away with him? I knew that Mum and Dad would definitely not welcome him in our vicinity. I was in a dilemma. I felt I had to choose between him or my parents. After much thought and consideration, I decided I had to put my parents first. I needed to tell John his six weeks at sea to come to New Zealand had been a waste of time. That was the hardest part. My heart was breaking as I broke the news to him that I had another boyfriend. Not true, of course, but it was the only way I could separate him from me. We met up a couple more times before he told me he had decided to go to Australia and work his way round the country. This second break up seemed even more painful than the first one. I never really got over it. I tried dating other boys, but it didn't work out. The first one was a Maori boy I'd met at a pub one evening, Webster. He seemed good fun and we'd go out with a group of work colleagues at the weekends. One day he invited me to go and meet his family who lived 'out in the sticks' somewhere.

"We'll go for the weekend," he said. "They'd love to meet you. There's my mum and dad, aunt and uncle and a couple of cousins".

We arrived at this wooden shack in the middle of nowhere, by a river, on a Friday evening. Lots of excitement about meeting Webster's new girlfriend, particularly as she was from England!

"We'll go and catch some eels from the river in the morning," Webster said. "We can have them for our tea." This did not appeal to me at all, but I decided to be hospitable and go along with it. The next morning, I sat on the riverbank whilst Webster fished for eels. He caught many and we took them back to the shack. "We're having a party tonight," he smiled. "Lots of people coming. Good music and good food." I didn't know what to expect but I knew it would be noisy. We had eaten some eels for tea and a couple of hours later I had stomach ache. "Go and have a lie down," suggested Webster, "you'll feel better later."

I did, but I didn't feel better. I was in agony. All I could hear was this loud music and lots of talking and laughter. It was going right over my head and I was dizzy with pain, almost going unconscious. In the end I couldn't speak, and Webster said if I didn't feel better in the morning he would get me to a doctor. Next morning, I was bundled into the car and driven to the nearest doctor. I almost collapsed in the waiting room. The doctor was shocked at my condition and said that if I hadn't come to the surgery that morning then I may have died in the afternoon! I had very severe food poisoning. It had been a very close shave. All I wanted to do was go home. After taking the medication the doctor prescribed and having a rest, I was driven home. It wasn't Webster's fault but I lost all interest in seeing him again.

At work one day, my good friend, Carolyn, came over to me and said, "Christine, I'm thinking of getting a flat, I'd like to move out of home and be more independent. Do you want to come with me?"

The thought of not having the long bus journey to work each morning and evening certainly appealed to me. So did having a good time with a load of friends in a flat. "Yes, love to," I replied without any hesitation. "Let's start looking at the weekend." We did, and we found a suitable two-bedroom bungalow (or shack to be more precise) and I moved in soon after.

Our "Shack"

I enjoyed inventing new dishes using food I had never tried before; vegetable bean curry, spaghetti, pasta and noodle dishes. Our food at home had been very predictable. Mum and Dad liked their regular old-fashioned dishes and we always had the same seven-day routine: roast meat on a Sunday, cold meat on a Monday, cottage pie on a Tuesday, braising steak on a Wednesday, lamb or pork chops on a Thursday, fish on a Friday, and sausages on a Saturday.

Carolyn and I became friends with two Australian girls. They were such fun and told us where to go for the best parties.

"Hey, Carolyn and Christine, we are planning to travel around the islands, you know – hitchhiking. We're starting in Nelson, going fruit picking for a few weeks, and then on down to Christchurch. Why don't you guys come with us?"

We both thought it would be a wonderful experience, although I felt nervous at the prospect. "We could just go with them for the fruit picking in Nelson, couldn't we?" suggested Carolyn. "Take a month off work. It would be fun! Come on Christine, let's do it".

I felt a sense of excitement alongside a fear of the unknown. "Ok, I'll talk to Mum and Dad about it first," I said, and went home to discuss it.

I don't recall what Mum and Dad thought about the plan, but we decided to tell work we'd be gone for a month and off we went, initially on a train from Auckland down to Wellington, then a ferry across to Nelson. We were picked up by the owners of the fruit farm – a well known establishment that attracted pickers from overseas to "come and experience the real New Zealand!" Free accommodation and a small amount of cash for food was provided in exchange for working eight hours a day picking apples and pears. As we arrived, the vast orchards took our breath away.

"This is where you will sleep!" the owner shouted, whilst pointing a finger at a wooden shack. Neither of us spoke as we tumbled out of the car with our bags and, with some trepidation, opened the door to this dilapidated large shed with cracked windows and dirty floors.

"Where's the bathroom?" we asked, "and the toilet".

"Shower room down there on the left. Toilet is outside, look, over there."

We looked in the direction he was pointing. "I don't believe it," I whispered to Carolyn "It's a hole in the ground!"

The two Australian girls didn't seem phased at all. "We'll be fine," they said as they unpacked their bags. "Just need to focus on the positives.".

With a heavy heart we got ready for bed and contemplated whether this had been the biggest mistake of our lives. We had to go and buy our own food and, as we didn't have a car, this was an hour's walk to the nearest shops. "We'll just have to make the best of it," declared Carolyn. "We might meet some fun people tomorrow. It's an experience!"

"You need to be outside the shack at 6.30am ready and waiting for your pick up," the owners told us on our first day. "Don't be late!"

We were hustled into the back of a truck and bumped along through the orchards until we reached the trees with the ripe fruit. A sore and bruised bottom did nothing to cheer us up. As the hours went by, the ritual picking of the apples and pears was beginning to cause my fingers to blister. "Ah, you don't need to worry about that! You'll soon get used to it," the owners would tell us.

A few days later the novelty of fruit picking was beginning to wear thin. "What shall we do?" I said to Carolyn.

"Let's give it another week and then decide," she replied. "We can't just leave – we told them we'd be here for a month."

The fun we thought we would have was beginning to wear thin. Our spare time was spent walking the long trek into town to get food. Everyone was exhausted. We dreamed of having a bath, even a decent toilet. It was obvious we would have to leave, creep out under cover of darkness! I looked at the other three girls.

"Where shall we go then?"

"Can't go home, we told work we'd be gone for a month." The Aussie girls had already discussed it earlier. "We could always hitchhike down to Christchurch. That would be fun. Never been to Christchurch, have you guys?" Hitchhike? Me? Might be tricky, I thought, what if nobody picks us up. Where will we stay?

We hatched a plan and left very early in the morning before anyone was up. It was the first time I had done anything like this. Mum and Dad would definitely not have approved! Carolyn and I were soon picked up by a couple of boys, heading towards Christchurch and intending to stop in a hostel on the way down. Bob and Jim seemed pleased to have us travel with them, I thought they were somewhat raucous and loud, but we chatted and laughed as we drifted on down towards the south, wondering where we might end up. Nothing had been booked in advance, so we weren't sure if we'd be able to stay in this hostel. The boys seemed confident it would all be fine.

"Yeah, trust us girls, it's a great place, we've been there before." Carolyn seemed very at ease with everything, so I tried to let my worries and concerns go and enjoy the ride.

"Only got one bedroom left I'm afraid," said the guy on reception as we entered the hostel. "A double room with two single beds".

"Oh, we'll manage," replied Bob. "The girls can have the beds and us guys can sleep on the floor".

I couldn't believe my ears. It was agreed, so long as we paid for four people they would let us stay. After paying for one night, we all tumbled into the room and I thankfully laid my head down on the pillow and went straight to sleep. Waking early at about 6.30am, I opened my eyes to see the boys had gone. "Goodness, the boys have left!" I woke Carolyn with the news.

"Maybe they just went for breakfast," she muttered, sitting up. "Come on, we better go too." As I went to my bags, I noticed the zip had been opened. I stared in disbelief as I realised that one of the boys had been into my bag. My purse was missing!

I screamed out, "Carolyn! They've taken my money!"

We ran outside, still in our night wear, and saw the car had gone. We were both devastated. "How could they do this to me?" I sobbed. "What shall we do now?"

We were both hungry and had no money to buy any food. We went to the local shop and asked if we could use their telephone to ring our parents. Then we asked if we could have some fruit and bread and that we would bring the money in later. They agreed. I managed to get through to Dad to tell him everything that had happened. I thought he would be furious with me, but he understood my predicament and felt sorry for me. "Don't worry dear," he said, "I won't tell your mother, she will only fret and worry. I will send some cash by special delivery to the post office there, and you need to get the first train home. You can explain everything to Mum when you return home."

With huge relief I checked in at the post office in the afternoon. The money had arrived. I was going home! I can't remember whether Carolyn returned with me or whether she carried on to Christchurch, but when Mum heard about everything that happened she almost had a fit. She was so relieved I was home.

"Anything could have happened to you!" she raged, "Very silly to go off like that, with boys you never met. Stupid!"

One thing that really inspired me whilst living in New Zealand was my love for Maori music. I bought LP records and listened and sang to them most days. There is something about Polynesian music that resonates with me and this has continued to the present day. Little did I know then that I would be reengaging with Polynesian music in a different country thirty years later.

"Why don't we take a weekend off and go visit Rotorua?" Mum said one day. "Everyone says how beautiful it is – all those steaming bubbling pools and a peep at real Maori traditions."

For once Dad agreed. Travelling around at weekends was not Dad's choice of relaxation – he much preferred to be on his boat and potter round the beach.

We chose a weekend where we would all be free to go. It certainly was an incredible experience. When I look back at the photos of that weekend I realise how lucky we were to have been able to wander around this ancient land. The smell of sulphur dominated the air as we visited the bubbling mud pools, geysers, hot thermal springs, and we were treated to a beautiful dance by some local Maori girls. I'm sure these days the place is more touristy and commercial and I am grateful that we saw the place in its relatively raw state.

Now that I was living independently in our flat, Carolyn and I often took off on adventures with anyone who wished to accompany us. Camping on beaches up and down the coast was a favourite of ours, although we sought a bit of fun, not solitude.

One of my diary entries reads: We found a beautiful beach not far from our camping area, but there was nobody on it, so we left.

I was enjoying a succession of fleeting relationships with different boys, met at parties or friends of friends. One of them, Harry, was to become my boyfriend for a while – in fact until we eventually left Auckland. He was tall, good fun and seemed completely besotted with me. I was still mourning for John, so I regarded him more of a close friend. We spent most weekends together and Mum and Dad gradually

Living the good life

got to know and like him. He liked to take me home to his family, a 'typical New Zealand' family where Mum made the scones and Dad ruled the roost. Gradually, I think Harry was convinced I would marry him.

As the months went by Dad became increasingly frustrated and unhappy in his job, but there were no other job opportunities that inspired him. Eventually it was realised that the money that was coming into the household would never be enough to pay the fare to bring my nana over to visit, and after nearly three years Mum was feeling very homesick and missing her. Added to this, Jonathan's education was being stifled. The school he attended was very limited regards opportunities, he was literally being held back from progressing. The only one who didn't want to return to England was Julia, who had fallen in love with a local boy, Philip.

Sometime later arrangements were made to return. It was with a heavy heart that Dad gave notice and booked our passage home on the same ship that had brought us there - the Angelina Lauro. Harry was heartbroken and asked if he could come with us – provided I would marry him. I declined his offer, yet he insisted on travelling with us as far as Brisbane. I felt so sorry for him, but I was not in love with him and I couldn't pretend to be. Philip proposed to Julia and she accepted. Philip said he would come as soon as we had found accommodation in England. Carolyn was very upset I was leaving but she promised to come and visit us once we were settled back home. I gave notice at work and realised how much I would miss all my lovely friends from the Auckland Savings Bank. We'd had such fun together. I was very touched when I found out they made me a tape recording of good wishes to take home with me.

By now we had acquired a cat, rescued from the local neighbourhood. Cats were never treated kindly in New Zealand – most people saw them as pests and only kept them to catch mice and rats. We had become fond of this one, so we booked a passage for him - as well as Fluffy of course! We knew that both of them would have to endure six months quarantine when they arrived back in the UK – a regulation in those days.

Of course the main priority for Dad was to find a suitable and satisfying job back in England. He'd kept in touch with colleagues from Colston, particularly the service manager. Fortunately, they were looking for an administrative manager for the office of the service division. The pay was not brilliant, but Dad was happy to accept. Our house and furniture were quickly sold, and we left with our personal belongings and the animals in May 1969. Bands were playing on the quayside and streamers were flying everywhere as we stood on the decks, sadly watching Wellington fade into the distance.

The Suez Canal had been closed due to conflict in the Middle East, so our return journey entailed travelling via Sydney, Brisbane, Adelaide, Perth, Cape Town, Tenerife and on to Southampton. I remember alighting from the ship in Brisbane and the heat hit me like a blast from a furnace. How do people live in a place like this permanently? I thought to myself. Next stop Adelaide where we took ourselves off to a local zoo in the time we had available to us. On to Perth and then to Cape Town which, being 5,600 miles, meant we were on board ship for twelve consecutive days. Nothing but sea, sea, sea. There were flying fish to be seen, then dolphins occasionally ducking and diving around the ship. Eating, walking the dog on the dog deck, reading, sunbathing. That was our daily life. Finally, the Cape of Good Hope came into view and what an amazing spectacle to behold! Table Mountain rose from the land like another planet, it took hours of sailing before we finally docked in Cape Town. We were hoping for a cable car ride up Table Mountain, but it had been closed due to poor visibility.

We had a full day ashore so, having decided to go shopping, buy postcards and post them back home, we made our way to a post office. There were two long queues. One for the 'Whites' and one for the 'Blacks'. This was something I had only heard about on the news and to experience standing in a separate line because of the colour of our skin felt very strange to me. It was virtually unheard of to see anyone of 'mixed race'. I was glad to leave Cape Town and looked forward to our next, and last, port of call – Tenerife. It was becoming a 'hot spot' for tourists, but

Thrilled to be back with my Nana (in the deckchair), my cousin Jennifer on Mum's knee

nothing on the scale it is today. Three days later we arrived in Southampton, mid July to a wonderful welcome by my nana, my Auntie Iris, and daughter Jennifer. Our old neighbour, Mrs Brooks, was also there to greet us and offered us accommodation for our first few days back in old Pommy Land.

We all felt a sense of relief, excitement, and a certain amount of fear for the future. Where would we live? How would Dad's job work out? Would I like my new surroundings, make new friends, enjoy a new job? All quite scary. Our family had stuck together through thick and thin, we had become extremely close and we would all move forward together.

The first step in arriving back to England was to find accommodation near High Wycombe where Dad would be commuting to work.

"Well, I'm not very keen on living in High Wycombe," Mum had declared after looking around. "It's too sprawling and miles from anything!"

A tour of the surrounding areas brought us to the Thames area outside Reading, near to where we had lived in Sonning years previously.

"Maidenhead, yes, that's the place! Near to the river, good shopping facilities, good schools and lovely countryside." So, Maidenhead it was. A modern detached house in Bloomfield Road, much smaller than our house in Auckland.

Only three bedrooms so I had to share a room with Julia and Karen, not something I was thrilled about.

I immediately started searching for a suitable job, as did Julia. I found one in Cookham, about twenty minutes by bus, at ICL (International Computers Ltd). Cookham is a beautiful little village on the Thames, it still had the old apothecary in the high street and the butchers and greengrocers – long since closed. I had applied for a junior secretarial role which meant working for one of the managers in a small office with another girl called Rita. I found the work pretty boring and less relaxed than my experience of office work in Auckland. I remember being admonished for being too friendly with the manager – meaning I should speak to him as my superior rather than a work colleague - something that felt alien to me after working with Kiwis for so long.

Bloomfield Rd.

Karen was sixteen and had no qualifications behind her. She had returned from Auckland slightly overweight and, in her attempt to slim down and be attractive to the boys, she had gone on an extremely strict diet. Almost anorexic. I knew Mum and Dad were worried about her. She was not eligible for the sixth form at school, having no GCE's behind her. Mum persevered with the local authorities and eventually got her into Maidenhead High School where she obtained sufficient qualifications to enter teacher training college where she qualified as a teacher.

Jonathan had learned virtually nothing in school in New Zealand yet his previously pressurized education in prep school qualified him to be accepted into Maidenhead Grammar School.

Meanwhile Dad started work in High Wycombe, with some of the same colleagues he had left behind three years earlier! He was included in managerial meetings and his previous knowledge and experience was an advantage to him.

My social life took off when I decided to join the Young Conservatives. There wasn't much going on in Maidenhead, and when someone suggested I go along to one of their meetings I decided it was better than nothing. As it happens I met some very eligible young men there, there were dances, meals out and I quickly made some new friends. As we had brought Fluffy back on the ship with us, most weekends were spent travelling to visit him in quarantine – a journey of about an hour. He was there for six months, poor dog. It was a wonderful day when we finally went to collect him.

A few months later I heard from my dear friend, Carolyn, from New Zealand. A letter arrived though the door one day. It read:

Dear Christine, I've given it much thought and I've decided to come over to England and visit you. I've always wanted to come to Europe and I'm saving up enough money to travel around a bit. Will that be ok with you?

I was thrilled. I'd missed her a lot and I knew she would have fun going to events and parties with me.

At the same time, we got a note from the Knott family in Auckland, who'd been our close friends out there. They were touring Britain in a camper van and, "would it be all right to park in your drive for a bit?" This they did – for longer than was comfortable for us.

Carolyn came and stayed for a few weeks until she felt confident enough to go off travelling by herself. We lost contact for a short while, then eventually she returned to tell me that she had met "a new fabulous boy" and that their relationship was very serious. It wasn't long before they married. Carolyn had decided to stay in England for the foreseeable future.

Very soon Julia's boyfriend Philip arrived to be reunited with his fiancé. We were getting used to Kiwis landing on our door step; fortunately, Mum was a very outgoing sociable person who never seemed to mind. Their engagement lasted until 1971 when they planned their wedding for the summer of the following year. As it happened I met my future husband, Ken, at the same time and our wedding was also arranged for the summer of 1972

Wedding day

- in the beautiful village of Cookham. The reception on a barge on the Thames.

Unfortunately, we couldn't afford to buy any kind of property in the Maidenhead area, so Ken applied for a job elsewhere and accepted one in Weymouth, Dorset. We moved into a delightful two-bedroom bungalow immediately after the wedding and I found a new job with the Abbey National Building Society as a secretary. I was terribly homesick for the first year or so and yearned to return to Berkshire. This was going to be a new era for me, like it or not!

EPILOGUE

After six months of marriage Ken and I decided to move from Weymouth to Wiltshire and we settled in Corsham. I worked for a building society in Bath until I gave up work two years later to give birth to our first child, a beautiful daughter, Lucy. Two and a half years later we were gifted with another baby, this time a boy. Jeremy was born in 1977. I decided not to go back to work whilst the children were young, partly because I had begun to have some health problems and struggled with Chronic Fatigue but also, I didn't feel comfortable leaving my two precious children in the care of someone I did not know. In 1981 we moved to Berkshire to be near my parents. I felt I needed some support. A short time later, I trained in complementary therapies and studied healthy living alternatives. This was essential for me as I struggled to get out of bed each morning and take care of the children. It helped a great deal and I am still involved with this to the present day. I then went on to study child psychology and counselling.

Julia and Philip had four boys and lived in Maidenhead. Karen also lived in Maidenhead where she married and had four children. Tragically, her life was cut short in 1994 after suffering with a brain tumour for several years. She was 41. This obviously had a devastating effect on us all, but her four children have all grown up to be happy independent beings. Jonathan married and moved to Cambridge, he had two girls. Mum and Dad who were living close to the Thames, bought a little boat and regularly enjoyed sailing down the river on summer weekends yet they struggled with health issues, never having really recovered from Karen's death. Dad began to lose his sight at age 80 and Mum struggled with this situation for four years until she died of a stroke in 2003, age 79. Dad passed away nine months later. He wrote his autobiography before he died but only gave copies to the family. Recently, Jonathan has extracted the war years from his book and had it published on Amazon, "Scuppers to Skipper" – which has sold over 1000 copies to date.

Julia and Philip emigrated to New Zealand with the family, shortly after Mum and Dad died. Ken and I encountered problems in our marriage in the 1990's and we divorced in 2002. Since the divorce, I have moved to Sussex and started travelling again. Jonathan was based in California for a few years, working in Silicon Valley. I visited him there in the late nineties and met a variety of people, one of whom I stayed in touch with for a couple of years. His name was Dwight, who subsequently moved to the Big Island of Hawaii. I visited him soon afterwards and had the wonderful opportunity of getting to know the best beaches to swim with the dolphins, the sacred sites, the places of historical interest, and more. I felt I wanted to share this with other people, so the following year I decided to take a group of people over there and give them a ten-day tour of the Island. This also gave me the cash to pay my air fare and accommodation. It began to feel like my spiritual home and I continued with being a 'tour guide' for six years. A much-needed opportunity to get away from the English winter for a few weeks! I made many friends there over the years and have continued to visit the island whenever I can.

I have also spent time in California, exploring incredible places such as the Yosemite National Park and Mt. Shasta. In 2007 I travelled around New Zealand. My daughter, Lucy, and husband. Mike, along with their baby, Louis, were attending a family wedding in Wellington, so after a brief spell there, I went down to Christchurch (before the earthquake!) to Mt. Cook, and up to Auckland – where my mission was to investigate some family history at the Military Museum there.

My interest in genealogy goes back many years. I was given much information by my second cousin, John, who lives in Nottingham. Yet there were gaps and I have been actively seeking to fill these gaps whenever I can. My mother, Thelma Bishop, told me a lot about the Bishop side of the family but it wasn't until 2012 when the BBC, having seen my family tree on a website, contacted me asking for information about the Bishop family, that I was able to complete the family tree. In their programme Who Do You Think You Are they were featuring the well known comedian John Bishop and to my astonishment I discovered that I was related to him. I knew that my grandfather, Ernie Bishop, had a brother called Fred, but I don't ever recall meeting him on our frequent visits to Liverpool. The reunion of this extended family turned out to be a memorable occasion for us all. John and his family remain in touch with us. The programme itself focussed on our great-great-grandfather, Charles Bishop, the very person Mum used talk about when I was a child. When we lived near Chichester, she would say, "Look over there at the Cathedral, that's where Charles Bishop used to sing you know." He was also a lay clerk. He was a well-known singer from around 1850 to 1880 when he toured, living at various places around the UK, including singing at York Minster, New College, Oxford, and then Liverpool. He even joined the Black & White Minstrels and toured America. So, for me, to see this tale coming to life on a BBC programme was very emotional. As for Uncle Eddie

Bishop, whom we met on the ship in Melbourne in 1966, he could never have foreseen that his brother, Fred, would have a grandson called John who became one of Britain's top comedians.

A few years ago the nation watched a TV programme that involved John cycling around the south of Australia for charity. The programme was intended to replicate the journey he made many years ago - long before he ever dreamed about becoming a comedian - when he'd raised a huge amount for good causes. When I sat down to watch it imagine my surprise and astonishment when I learned that his final stop on his trip would be to visit the place where Uncle Eddie, our mutual Gt.Uncle, had lived and where, still, many people could remember the kind soul he was. The cameras took us up the winding tracks from Melbourne through deserted land until it finally reached the town where Eddie lived. John spoke to people who remembered him and I felt very emotional as John visited his grave and placed a bouquet of flowers on behalf of his family. I just wished Mum had still been around to watch too. The 'icing on the cake' was – for me – a photo John had been handed by an old friend of Eddie. It turned out to be the polaroid photo I had taken on the ship in 1966! On John's return to England the photo was put in the post and returned to me. I was totally overcome by that gesture, I will treasure it always.

My reference to the fact that Percy Edney may not have been Dad's real father came about when I read his autobiography in more detail after he died. Dad mentioned Ernest Walling, a man he had never met but who had sent him birthday and Christmas presents for his first 25 years. Ernest was an insurance clerk and a writer of children's stories and lived in Rotherhithe. My grandmother was lodging with him whilst Percy was away in the Army towards the end of the First World War. My grandmother and Percy married just six months before Dad was born in October 1918. I believe Dad inherited Ernest' capacity for good writing and an ability to reach high grades in Maths, which enabled him to become an officer in the navy. Several years ago I traced a grandson of Ernest who sent me a photo of him and there was an uncanny likeness to Dad. We'll never know for sure.

I am now enjoying spending time with my five grandchildren, Josh, Dylan, Sophia, Louis, and Tom, who live fairly close. I am particularly interested in exploring a more unconventional lifestyle, engaging in activities that can access more opportunity for awareness, including meditation and mindfulness in my daily life. I've not eaten meat for over thirty years and I regularly campaign for humanity towards animals. I have done many training courses: Massage, Shiatsu, Transpersonal Psychology, Life Coaching, Personology (Face Reading), Teaching English as a foreign Language. I'm a member of a local writing group, enjoy reading books of all genres - mainly non-fiction, philosophy, and psychology. I enjoy authors such as Paulo Coelho, Bill Bryson, and Winston Graham. I help co-ordinate a befriending group for the elderly and I like dance, attending workshops, music, and coastal walks. . I also have a sweet cat called Daisy. Daisy has her own Facebook page and (with my help) likes to write her own 'blogs'. She sees life, the world and my personal life as a source of amusement and, it would seem, many people enjoy reading her reflections. My family has expanded considerably since Mum and Dad passed away. They would be very proud of all their great-grandchildren –

twenty in total, ages range from two months to twelve. Six live overseas but I enjoy spending time whenever possible with the other fourteen.

I live close to the Ashdown Forest and a village called Forest Row. I think 'fate' brought me here! I feel fortunate in being able to access numerous interesting events, talks, workshops and gatherings that are often absent in other parts of the country. Certainly, when I left Wokingham in 2006, having lived there for twenty-four years, there was nothing I missed. My life here is very rich in terms of good friends and a close community. I have been able to connect with like-minded people, and further my interests in writing, philosophy, healthy-living – the list is endless. The subject of epigenetics has interested me for a while now and there are new discoveries all the time. If I could go back to being a teenager, I would certainly go to university and study epigenetics.

My main reason for writing this book was not only to tell my own story, but to continue where Dad left off. His book, Scuppers to Skipper which describes his war years (in some detail) has inspired and informed people of the role his generation played in keeping our country safe. I feel lucky to have been born to someone who survived it all. His legacy lives on and his descendants have a part to play in continuing it. Although Dad hardly ever mentioned the war whilst I was growing up, my Mum talked about it quite a lot – telling me that it was his determination and fortitude that got him through. He would never take no for an answer and always found a way to climb over any hurdles that prevented him moving forward. As a daughter, I found him to be particularly harsh when it came to discipline and we children had to learn to 'toe the line' as it were. He wouldn't stand for any excuses or feeble sad sob stories. Deep down, I admired him for these qualities, although if it wasn't for Mum and her easy-going attitude, we would have certainly been squashed when it came to self-expression and flexibility. Despite all of this I knew he loved us and would do anything for us. I think I have inherited some of his determination and fortitude, although my mother's influence has softened my approach to others.

Christine's 70th Birthday Party with children and grandchildren

Everyone is different and thank goodness for that!

Family Tree

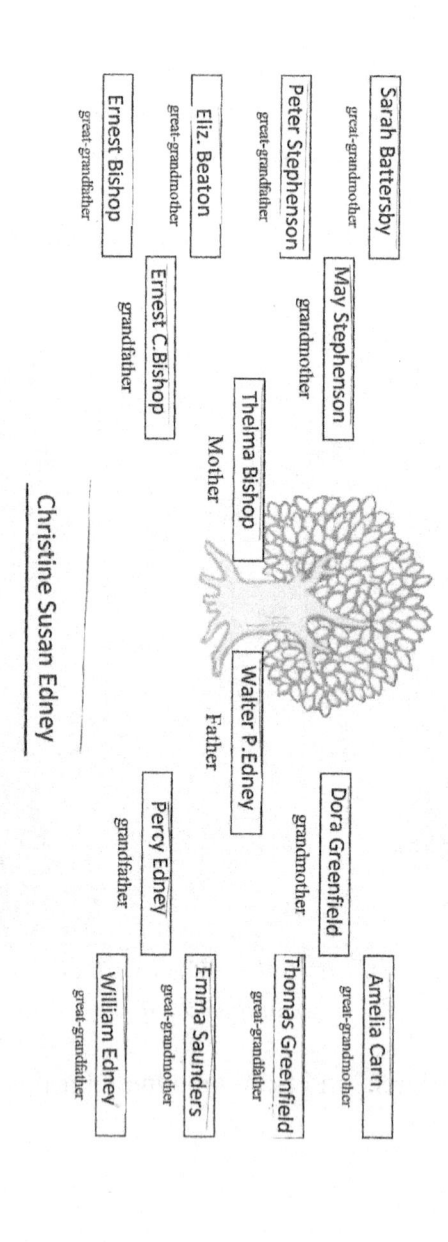

- Sarah Battersby — *great-grandmother*
- Peter Stephenson — *great-grandfather*
- Eliz. Beaton — *great-grandmother*
- Ernest Bishop — *great-grandfather*
- May Stephenson — *grandmother*
- Ernest C. Bishop — *grandfather*
- Thelma Bishop — Mother
- Walter P. Edney — Father
- Dora Greenfield — *grandmother*
- Percy Edney — *grandfather*
- Amelia Carn — *great-grandmother*
- Thomas Greenfield — *great-grandfather*
- Emma Saunders — *great-grandmother*
- William Edney — *great-grandfather*

Christine Susan Edney

Made in the USA
Middletown, DE
19 May 2023